THE WEDDING SPEECH MANUAL

THE COMPLETE GUIDE TO PREPARING, WRITING AND PERFORMING YOUR WEDDING SPEECH

PETER OXLEY

Published by Peter Oxley

License Notes

Peter Oxley

Contents

List of Exercises

***

Chapter 1 - Introduction

So you're going to make a speech at a wedding: congratulations! You're about to embark on an experience that, if you approach it right, can be a rewarding experience that you'll remember for the rest of your life – and for all the right reasons!

Many people dread doing a wedding speech, not knowing where or how to start and what they should say. For some this can take over their preparations and become something which, at its worst, can ruin their enjoyment of the day itself.

You are not alone if you feel this way: public speaking is often listed as one of the biggest fears people have, above even death, heights and spiders! Indeed, the first thing to realise is you are not alone: many others, probably some in your own wedding party, will be feeling exactly the same way.

The next thing is to be reassured: you don't have to feel this way. There are a few simple techniques which can help you to not only beat your nerves, but also write your speech and present it in a way which comes across as professional, assured and confident.

I came across these techniques during one particularly hectic year when I spoke at two weddings just a couple of months apart: first as the groom and then the best man. Fearful of standing up with nothing to say and making a fool of myself as a result, I tried all the books and other sources I could find to get to grips with what to say and how to say it.

However, I found that the best preparation lay in what I already knew: my experiences and training in business, spending years presenting to not only small groups of directors round a boardroom table but also hundreds of disgruntled employees on the factory floor.

I realised that writing and making a wedding speech was really not much different from what I'd learnt and put into practice over all those years. Doing the speeches proved this theory right. In fact, I was surprised how easy it all was.

In this book I will share with you those secrets and show you:

- How to prepare properly and when to start.
- What you will be expected to say.
- How to ensure nerves don't get the better of you.
- How to ensure that your speech works for your audience.
- How to get the material you'll need for your speech.
- How to write your speech.
- How to deliver your speech confidently and professionally.

How to use this book

This book has been designed with all types of wedding speech maker in mind and can be used in a number of different ways:

> • If you're a complete beginner (or just that way inclined), you can read it in the traditional way, starting at the beginning and working your way through to the end. Each section has been designed as not just a guide on how to do it, but also with exercises to lead you through the process, step-by-step. If you follow these in order, you'll find that in no time and with much less effort than you probably thought you'll be fully prepared and ready to stand up and make that speech.

> • If you feel happy with certain elements of the process, but not so sure about others, you can just read the relevant sections. Below is a list of all the chapters with a short summary of what is included, so you can pick and choose as you see fit. All chapters are designed to be self-contained, so while it's useful in one way to read them in order, I won't be offended if you decide to skip around – promise!

> • Likewise, you can dip in and out of whichever sections you want whenever you want. There are many areas which are useful to general public speaking, or even just confidence building, and so you will no doubt find yourself referring back to this time and again, long after the wedding is over.

> • Exercises are set out throughout the book which will help you to progress your speech. Complete these in order and you will be a long way towards your finished wedding speech!

> • If you find yourself grappling with a specific issue, try using the Troubleshooting section at the end of this book. This includes many of the common problems which can arise, with tips on how to deal with them or avoid them altogether.

The importance of personal content

One thing I truly believe is that wedding speeches which are made up of plenty of relevant, personal material are always better than a collection of off-the-peg one-liners.

It can be very tempting to rely on tried and tested gags and jokes to fill your speech and get people laughing. While you shouldn't avoid these altogether, you should use them in moderation.

One or two lines are great to give you an easy laugh, but too many and you'll leave your audience unsatisfied. Remember: you've been asked to speak because of who you are. Because of your relationship with the happy couple, they have entrusted you with the job of providing the audience with some nice, entertaining insights to their lives.

This book will show you how to build and deliver a speech tailored to the individual circumstances of your particular happy day. This in turn will give you a personal, entertaining speech which (a) no-one else could have done and (b) will be remembered by all those present, for all the right reasons!

***

Chapter 2 - The Speeches

Before we start thinking about what to say and how to say it, it's worthwhile spending a bit of time considering what the speeches are supposed to achieve, when they should be and what you as a speechmaker are expected to say.

2.1 The order of the speeches

This section is mainly aimed at those who have an active role in organising the wedding, which will usually be the bride and groom and possibly also their parents. However, if you're the best man or have some other role then there's no harm in being aware of the various options: you could earn some brownie points by being able to provide some sensible advice or thoughts if needed!

If you're organising a wedding, then it's largely up to you how many speeches you have and when they are.

Traditionally there will be three: the father of the bride, followed by the groom and then the best man. In many weddings these will come at the end of the wedding breakfast and before the evening's celebrations begin, marking a dividing line between the formal part of the day and the less formal (or more fun?) part.

You don't need to follow this format if you don't want to. For example:

- I've been to weddings where the speeches were held before the meal, to allow the speechmakers to enjoy the meal without the speeches hanging over them.

- At my wedding, we spread the speeches out, one after each course of the meal, to reduce the risk of "speech fatigue" among the guests.

If you feel that it is more appropriate to use a different order, there's no law which says you can't change things. The important thing is that you are all comfortable with the order, that it works, and makes sense.

In deciding how many speeches to have and when they should be, consider the following:

> • The comfort and attention span of your guests: if you leave all the speeches to the very end of the meal, remember they will have been sitting for a long time and be itching to hit the dance floor. You should therefore avoid long, drawn-out speeches without comfort breaks.

> • This especially applies to the number of speeches you have. For example, it's becoming more and more common for others to say some words (such as the bride, or the groom's parents). I would caution strongly against having too many speeches: the longer the speeches go on, the more likely you are to bore and even irritate your guests.

> • The expectations of your guests: if you're having a very traditional wedding, it may make sense to ensure everything follows a traditional format.

> • The preferences of the organisers and the logistics of the day. At my wedding, having a speech after every course meant we needed to make sure there was some tight co-ordination and communication with the kitchen and waiting-on staff. Make sure you discuss your thoughts with the organisers and the venue to make sure that what you want to do will actually work.

2.2 The purpose of the speeches

Although there are in theory no limits to what you can say in your speech (apart from of course taste, decency and the audience's sense of humour), there are certain things which you will be expected to say.

The below are intended to give you an introduction to the general areas to include. For full and detailed speech outlines, see chapter 7.

Father (or mother) of the Bride

Traditionally the father of the bride will speak about his daughter, but it is becoming more common for the mother to also say something along similar lines. In a symbolic way, this is the parents' last act before their daughter begins her new life with her new husband. In times gone by this was the father handing over the responsibility for looking after his daughter.

You should:

> • Take the opportunity to talk about your daughter (in particular, say nice things about her).
>
> • Give some insights into her past (and what her husband is letting himself in for!).
>
> • Set the scene for the rest of the day.
>
> • Thank people for attending, helping to organise the day, etc.
>
> • Toast the bride and groom.

The Groom

If you're following a traditional order of ceremonies, then the purpose of the groom's speech is to respond to the father of the bride's speech, thanking him for his words, and saying something about his new wife.

Don't be afraid to gush and be romantic here: this is the one time when your mates won't rib you (too much) for it, you'll earn some big brownie points, and get everyone in the audience on your side.

You should:

> • Respond to the father of the bride's speech and thank him for his words (i.e. the speech he has just made in which he was (hopefully!) complimentary about you).
>
> • Thank everyone for coming.
>
> • Thank them for their gifts and well-wishes.
>
> • Thank anyone who helped pay for the day and / or were involved in the organising and running of the day.
>
> • Thank the bridal party for performing their roles: i.e. the bridesmaids, best man, ushers, etc. You may wish to give them

presents as a thank you for their roles. This could be a useful part of your speech: a good way to fill time if you're afraid that you don't have enough to talk about. Alternatively you could hand out the presents at a different time, especially if you're worried about the speeches going on for too long.

• Talk about how you met your wife, your relationship, your life together and how you feel about her and being married to her. In particular, don't forget to say nice things about her.

• End on a toast: traditionally to the bridesmaids.

The Best Man

Typically this will be the best or oldest friend of the groom, possibly someone he trusts to not completely humiliate him (!). Given that the other speeches have been all about the bride, this speech is usually all about the groom: giving an insight to who he is and providing some humorous stories from his past.

A word of caution. It's almost universally accepted that the best man will humiliate the groom and, done in the right way, this can be a speech to remember. However, in doing so you should be good-natured, definitely not vindictive, and make sure you don't step over the line. In thinking about where "the line" is, don't just think about the bride and groom's reactions, but also your audience (see chapter 5 below): they need to find it funny too, otherwise you'll get them offside and, as comedians say, "die the death". Trust me: you don't want this to happen.

You should:

• Respond to the groom's speech, thanking him for his words (and any gifts) on behalf of the bridal party.

• Read out any messages / cards from people who were not able to be there.

• Compliment the bride on how she looks.

• Tell some humorous anecdotes about the groom.

• If you are the last speaker, introduce the evening's entertainment.

The Maid of Honour or Other Bridesmaids

Not a traditional speech as such, but more and more weddings include time for the maid of honour to also say some words. You should:

> • Respond to the groom's speech, thanking him for his words (and any gifts) on behalf of the bridal party.
>
> • Compliment the bride on how she looks.
>
> • Provide some insights on the bride from the perspective of her friends.
>
> • Welcome the groom to your circle of friends.
>
> • If you are the last speaker, introduce the evening's entertainment.

The Wedding Effect

Bear in mind your bride's sensitivities here and avoid taking the Mickey out of her unless (a) you're really sure she will find it funny and (b) it's nothing too close to the bone or humiliating. If in doubt, check. Actually, check even if you have no doubts.

You may have always known her to be up for a laugh, but don't underestimate The Wedding Effect. Even the most laid-back and "laddish" of women will have harboured dreams of their special day since they were a little girl: looking like a princess, everyone fussing over them, etc., etc.

Even the smallest careless word could hurt her and ruin her day, so the biggest and most important piece of advice I can give you is to play it safe. The one thing most likely to lose you the goodwill of your audience (and in particular her friends and family) is upsetting your bride. This applies to all the speeches, so fathers of the bride and – especially – best men, also take note!

That said, tears of joy are good and if you want a target to aim for, getting her to well up with tears as a result of the beauty of your words is a good one to have (I particularly enjoyed playing this game: get her going and just watch the other women in the room follow suit!). You should not be afraid to ladle it on thick here and be gushy and romantic: even if you are in front of all your mates. You will reap dividends in terms of the reactions of the audience, not to mention that of your new wife.

What all the speeches should include

Aside from saying nice things about the bride (see "The Wedding Effect" above), you'll see that thank yous are a common theme and here's a quick tip for you. A great way to start your speech, whether you're the father of the bride, groom or best man, is to thank people and then lead the applause.

This has a few big benefits:

- They're easy words to write and remember.

- They get everyone on your side.

- Most importantly everyone will be clapping while you're standing there talking - this all has an amazing effect on your confidence and will set you up nicely for the rest of your speech.

All speeches also traditionally end in a toast. Different people will have different ideas about what and who to toast. There are conventions and traditions as noted above, but if you'd like to do something differently that should be fine as long as you agree it with the organisers and the other speechmakers first to ensure that you don't all say the same thing.

Should I be funny?

A key role of the speeches is to provide the link between the serious, formal business of the day (the wedding and the wedding breakfast) and the fun, informal part (the dancing). The speeches are effectively the organisers' way of telling the guests that it's OK to now relax, have a laugh and have fun. An element of humour is therefore important, but don't get too obsessed with this.

There is increasing pressure these days for the speeches to be funny; indeed, this is often the source of many people's nerves at having to do the speech: worrying that they won't be funny enough.

Bear in mind that it is more important to keep the audience's attention and to entertain them than have them rolling in the aisles. Being funny is good, but it shouldn't be the be-all and end-all.

In particular you should avoid turning your speech into a series of one-liners, like a stand-up comedian. You may get some laughs but the audience will be left wanting more (not in a good way), wondering where the personal content was, the bit which told them something about the happy couple and the day they're enjoying. Remember: your job is to celebrate the people who you've all come to see: the newlyweds. If you think that a stand-up routine's needed, hire a comedian.

That's not to say you should shy away from humour altogether. Remember that you should be entertaining: humour is often a key part of this. Seek to balance this based on your own style, the people you are talking to, and the people you are talking about.

2.3 How long should they be?

You should again remember the audience's comfort and attention span. Even the best speech in the world can be a bore if it goes on for too long.

As a general rule I'd suggest you aim for five minutes maximum. This is long enough for you to say a decent amount of good stuff without boring everyone to tears.

Five minutes usually equates to about two or three pages of A4 paper if typed out with no blank lines between paragraphs. When you think of it this way, and remember that there is some formal stuff which you can throw in right away, then suddenly the job of writing the speech doesn't sound quite so bad!

Use the suggested five minutes as a guide: don't worry if you're a few minutes either side. If in doubt though, err on the side of making the speech shorter rather than longer. It's really hard to make a speech too short, but very easy to make it too long. Less is definitely more when it comes to wedding speeches. As long as you cover the key stuff, no-one will think you were too quick. However, rambling on and on over the same old points for the sake of filling time will be noticed and won't win you any friends!

A common question is whether five minutes is really enough for you to be able to say everything you want to say. There are two points to bear in mind here:

> • If you break it down, there are only a few key things that you really need to say (I love you / I'm proud of you / You're an

idiot sometimes but also my best mate...). Such things are so much more powerful if they are said in as few words as possible. The rest is just window dressing to entertain the crowd: but again remember that less is more!

• Don't forget that you are there to be entertaining, not to tell your life story. If there's more that you want to say, but can't fit it in to a short and entertaining speech, then take the bride and/or groom to one side afterwards and tell them separately.

2.4 Putting it into perspective

After reading this far you may be starting to worry about all the things you need to do or think about. How you can't possibly manage to do all this. How there's just too much to do.

It's perfectly natural to worry about these things, but you shouldn't worry. This book will take you through every step and make sure that in no time at all you'll be ready and raring to go.

It's very easy to overplay the importance of the speeches in the grand scheme of things. However, you should remember that they are only one part of the day.

The main purpose of the day is the wedding itself, and that the newlyweds and their family and friends have a good time. No-one ever went to a wedding just for the speeches.

A good speech will be remembered and talked about for a day or two afterwards. A bad speech has to be particularly bad to be remembered in years to come: follow the guidelines in this book and you can avoid making the sort of bad speech which is talked about for years to come, and will be all set to make a very good one!

We return to this theme when we think about nerves and how to deal with them in the next chapter: Reasons to Not be Fearful.

The Speeches: Summary of main points

• Traditionally, the speeches start with the father of the bride, followed by the groom and then the best man.

• There is, however, no reason why you shouldn't change this if you want to.

• Bear in mind the audience's comfort, expectations and the overall flow of the day.

• All speeches should include something complimentary about the bride – remember The Wedding Effect!

• Thanking people and leading a round of applause is a great way to start your speech, getting everyone involved (in a positive way) and giving you a nice confidence boost.

• Being funny is good, but don't overdo it. Avoid just having a speech full of off-the-peg one-liners: personalised content is best every time.

• Keep it in perspective: yes, you want to do a good job, but there are more important things going on that day…

***

Chapter 3 - Reasons to Not be Fearful

Often one of the biggest issues people have with making a wedding speech isn't researching or writing it, but the way they feel about standing up and talking in front of a room full of people.

I'm sure you've been there. I certainly have.

All of a sudden your heart starts beating hard and fast. The palms of your hands get clammy. You start to hyperventilate and sweat uncontrollably. Everything seems to go at a different pace. You feel unconnected from everything around you.

What's happening? Nerves. You may feel like you're the only one who suffers this way, but rest assured that that's far from the case. Think about the actor who suffers stage-fright (and believe me, they all do at one time or another): if this experienced professional can find themselves unable to do what they've trained so hard for, then what's the shame in you feeling a little nervous?

In this chapter we are going to think about nerves in the context of making a wedding speech:

> • Think about what nerves really are - the first and most important step towards winning a war is to know your enemy.

> • Think of why we let nerves affect us and, spinning it the other way, why you should not let them beat you.

> • Think about ways in which nerves can actually help you.

> • We will then look at techniques to master those pesky nerves.

3.1 What are nerves?

Put simply, nerves are an emotional and physical response to a stressful situation.

A lot of the things which result from nerves (such as increased heart rate, sweating, hyperventilating, etc.) are your body trying to bring in oxygen and generate energy to help you deal with a difficult situation. In times gone by it was to provide our ancestors with the energy and concentration to cope with a threat from a sabre-toothed tiger or other such predator: the so-called "fight or flight mechanism".

Therefore, your nerves are actually your body's way of trying to help you.

Everyone gets nervous. How successful they are in certain tasks depends (partly) on how they deal with those nerves.

Nerves should be seen as a positive thing: something which provides you with the energy to do your speech.

In addition, the increased adrenaline can help you think clearer, allowing you to perform at your optimum level.

3.2 Mastering your nerves

So your nerves are actually something intended to help, not hinder, you; but most people don't, or can't, think that way. This is mainly because when we think of being nervous we assume the worst: paralysed in front of a room full of people, fluffing or stuttering through our lines, visibly sweating and shaking.

It doesn't have to be that way.

The first step is to recognise your fears for what they are: your body trying to help you achieve your goal. What we need to do is turn all that energy into something positive.

Why are you afraid?

It's all very well me telling you that your nervousness is actually a good thing, but I bet you are probably thinking that that doesn't actually stop you being nervous!

Exercise 1 – Understanding why you are nervous

Take a piece of paper and draw a line down the middle, from top to bottom, splitting the page in two. At the top of the left hand side of the paper, write "Why am I nervous of making my speech?" Now take five minutes making a list of all of the answers to that question. Write down everything which comes into your head, no matter how big or small it seems. Feel free to bare your soul: you don't have to show this list to anyone if you don't want to.

Done? Now look back over your list. You'll probably find that at least one or two don't look quite so bad now you've written them down. There are probably one or two that you're already tempted to cross out because they really don't seem that important any more. Please resist this temptation for the moment.

The great thing about writing things down like this is that you can come to terms with them a lot better that way. If they're left to swill around your head, then the ideas get mixed up with your imagination and then get blown up out of all proportion. On the page, they are fixed and can't grow into little monsters.

Looking over the list, I now want you to think, for each point in your list: "Yes, but on the other hand..." For example, if you wrote: "No-one will laugh at my jokes," think instead: "But what if I use some really good jokes," or "They're my friends - of course they'll laugh!"

You've probably guessed what I'm going to ask you to do now. You're going to think of reasons not to be nervous. Write down your alternative, positive thoughts on the right hand side of the page. If you're stuck, try asking a friend / relative / colleague for their thoughts. I guarantee you'll get a response along the lines: "Don't be silly – of course that won't happen...!"

Take at least five minutes to do this. If you do it properly, I think you'll be pleasantly surprised at how many reasons not to be nervous that you can come up with.

Keep this list and refer back to it as the wedding day approaches. In preparing for your speech, focus on the positive thoughts on the right hand side, rather than the negative ones on the left hand side. Feel free to keep referring back to this list every time your nerves start getting the better of you.

Once you've done that, here are some more things to bear in mind.

What if it goes well?

Many of us tend to only think the worst: if we think the best will happen then we believe we're tempting fate and as a result nothing good will actually happen. I know I often fall into this trap.

It can be useful to assume the worst to ensure that you've covered all the angles in your preparation. It goes without saying though that this is likely to make your nerves worse, not better.

Rather than thinking that the glass is half-empty, imagine it as half-full. Spend a moment imagining the best possible outcome. Ignore all your fears. Picture a room full of cheering people, laughing and applauding. Everyone is proud of you: amazed that you have done such a professional-sounding, entertaining speech. You are the star of the moment.

A good feeling, isn't it? Store that feeling, that mental picture. You'll be using it a lot over the next few months. We go a lot more into Visualisation and Positive Mental Attitude a bit later in this chapter.

Get it in perspective

It's natural, as a speechmaker, to assume that your speech is the be-all-and-end-all of the day.

However, I've got some bad news for you. Sorry if I damage your ego, but there are one or two other things which are slightly more important than your speech and could actually ruin the day.

> • How about the wedding ceremony? If that doesn't happen, or gets interrupted, then that really would be a disaster (and your speech won't really be on anyone's mind by then...).

• What about the weather? Most couples dream of nothing but a bright, sunny day or crisp, white snow. Torrential rain and floods could really put a dampener on the day (pardon the pun…).

• The bride? Try telling any bride-to-be that your speech is more important than how she looks on the day (but only if you're wearing plenty of padding and preferably are as far away as possible!).

• The venue? We've all heard the horror stories of a wedding party turning up, only to be told they don't have a booking.

• The food? It would be terrible if everyone got food poisoning, wouldn't it?

• What if the band or DJ didn't turn up, or there was no champagne? Or…? (Hopefully you get the idea).

Now, bearing in mind all the above, think about how big a thing your speech is in the context of the whole day. Yes it is important. Yes, it deserves as much time and effort as possible so you do a great job. But keep it in perspective. As long as you don't leave the bride in tears (bad ones as opposed to tears of joy), or start a fist fight, you will really struggle to actually ruin the whole day.

Think about what you'll be doing: talking and telling a story, neither of which will be new skills for you. Indeed, these are things you'll have been doing since you were a toddler. The only thing that's different is the setting and the number of people you'll be speaking to.

Everyone will be on your side!

I really do mean this. No matter who you are, the majority - if not all - of your audience will want you to succeed.

Think back to when you've watched someone talk in front of a group of people and not done well. How did you, as an observer, feel? Embarrassed for them? Willing them to improve?

It's human nature to want people to do well.

Whatever you fear, or imagine, your audience aren't ogres. The vast majority of them will start from a position of wanting you to do well. Why wouldn't they?

If there are one or two people in the audience who you don't get on with, or who you really think will want you to fail: ignore them. They will be in the minority, trust me.

You will be well prepared!

Follow the tips in this book. Learn from any examples or advice that your friends and family give you. 99% of problems with speeches arise because the speechmaker did not prepare enough.

This will not apply to you. You will be fully prepared. Therefore, you'll be fine. Better than fine even - great!

Some other thoughts

Here are some other thoughts, specific to the various types of wedding speaker.

As the **father (or mother) of the bride**, you're going to be the one that everyone likes: you're giving away your daughter, someone you're very proud of. The audience will be made up of your family, friends, and friends of your daughter… You're on home territory: there's nothing to be afraid of!

Over the years I have seen plenty of extremely nervous fathers of the bride. Often it seems that they're in a worse state than the best man or even the groom!

I once spoke to a friend who was due to speak at his daughter's wedding. The guy was a confident person, well-liked by his friends and with a great sense of humour. Why then, I asked, was he so nervous?

"I've done some public speaking," he said, "but nothing quite like this. The main thing I'm worried about though is making a fool of myself in front of everyone. I don't want to let my daughter down."

As I explained to him, there really is no need to feel this way. In fact, the father of the bride is, in my opinion, the speaker with the least to worry about.

Everyone at the wedding will be on your side for a number of reasons:

• You're giving your daughter away: this is an emotional, important day for you and your family. As a result, you're going to be a very sympathetic character: it's a hard-hearted person who isn't on the side of the father of the bride.

• You're the host. If you don't think the fact that you're giving your daughter away isn't enough to get people rooting for you to do well, then I guarantee they will be rooting for their generous host to succeed.

• You'll be surrounded by your friends and family. I know that some families can be... let's say difficult, but on days like this families do pull together and support each other.

• As well as your daughter, her friends will naturally all be on your side: they're there because they care for her and so will care for you. They will support you because they want your daughter's day to be happy and special.

• Everyone will want you to succeed: especially if you're nervous, as there's nothing like knowing someone's nervous to make the audience want them to do well.

The important thing to remember is that you've got the easiest job of all the speechmakers. No-one really expects you to be funny: that's the best man's burden after all. Be touching and sincere about your daughter. If you also manage to make them laugh (and I'm sure you will), then that's a bonus.

As for my friend, the nervous father of the bride, his personality shone through (as I knew it would) and he did a highly successful speech and then sat down wondering why he'd been so nervous in the first place. You can too!

As **the groom (or indeed, the bride)**, it's your big day. People are there because they love you and want the day to go well for you. They are your friends and family (old and new): who'd not wish you well out of that lot?

I still remember how I felt when I realised that I was going to have to stand up in front of all my friends and family (plus many others) at my own wedding: dread, horror, constantly wondering what would happen if I messed up or embarrassed myself...

A lot of my friends and family had never seen me speak in front of a crowd before. Even though I was confident enough to know that I could do a good job, I still worried about freezing and making a fool of myself.

I didn't freeze, and only embarrassed myself when I hit the dance floor later that evening. Why? Because I was prepared and also remembered a few reasons why the groom, of anyone, can be confident of a great reception from everyone at their wedding.

- First off is an obvious one: it's your wedding day. Everyone's going to want you to do well and will want you to have the best possible day.

- You're one of the key people of the day: after the bride of course. Everyone will want the bride to have the perfect day. As her new husband, you'll benefit from that. They will be willing you to do the most amazing speech and so will be on your side all the way.

- In any case, pretty much everyone there will either be related to you or be your friend. That's probably the most sympathetic and supportive crowd you could ever hope for.

- It's only natural to worry about making a fool of yourself. But there are key ways to make sure you don't do that. Prepare and practise properly. Don't do or say anything you're not comfortable with. If you think a joke's not going to work, then don't use it.

At the end of the day, your role is simply to thank the father of the bride and the guests. The expectation for being hilarious lies on the best man. Anything you say or do to make people laugh is a bonus.

As **the best man**, it's forgivable to think that you've got the rough end of the stick, and in some ways you do. Sorry to break this to you, but (unlike the other speeches) the audience's expectations of your speech mean that you will have to be entertaining and funny.

Hot on the heels of my own wedding, I was called on to be best man at the wedding of two good friends of mine. I'd had a good confidence boost from speaking at my own wedding, but this was soon overtaken by nerves at needing to be as funny as possible.

However, I got through this by focusing on the positives. Although I didn't know as many people in the audience as I did at my own wedding, the groom and bride (the most important people) were on my side, as were the lads from the stag do.

If nothing else, I told myself, people will want to be entertained by you: that's the best man's job and that's their expectation. That may be a daunting thought, but look at it this way: they will be in a positive, welcoming frame of mind because:

> • It's a wedding and therefore a happy day,

> • The groom chose you as best man so there must be something good about you, and

> • They're looking forward to your speech so will be in a positive frame of mind: this is a great starting point for you!

At this point, in the interest of balance, I should talk here about how it's not actually that bad being the best man. How it really doesn't matter if you're not funny, or are inappropriate: how everyone will be on your side.

However, I don't want to lie to you. The best man's is the hardest out of the wedding speeches. In many cases you only really have the goodwill of your friends to draw on, while facing the stony glares of both sets of relatives.

There are some simple ways that you can generate goodwill and ensure the audience are on your side:

> • Use every opportunity to get to know people before you stand up to make your speech. Be nice, charming, vulnerable, own up to being nervous: anything to get them onside. At the stag do, get to know those people you don't know already.

> • Test your lines on as many people as possible to make sure that they are funny and appropriate.

> • Keep your speech personal, avoiding too many one-liners: you can't go far wrong if you deliver a heartfelt speech (peppered of course with the odd amusing anecdote) about how important the groom and his happiness are to you.

> • Make sure you are able to do the best possible job by practising your speech as much and as often as possible.

As **the maid of honour** you are a friend (maybe the best friend) of the bride, arguably the most important person on the day. As a result everyone will be on your side and wanting you to do well. In any case, people tend to be positively disposed towards bridesmaids at weddings.

Just like the best man, you will know the bride and groom as well as the girls from the hen do. However, unlike the best man you are not necessarily expected to be hilarious. As long as you stick to the points in this book to ensure you keep your speech short, entertaining and structured then you'll be fine. If you're funny, then great. But there's not necessarily any pressure for you to manage this: some kind and heartfelt words will work just as well.

As with the best man, there are some simple tricks you can use to ensure the audience are on your side:

> • Use every opportunity to get to know people before you stand up to make your speech. Be nice, charming, vulnerable, own up to being nervous: anything to get them onside. At the stag do, get to know those people you don't know already.

> • Road test your lines fully to make sure that they are funny and appropriate.

> • Keep your speech personal and avoid too many one-liners: you can't go far wrong if you deliver a heartfelt speech about how important the bride and her happiness are to you.

> • Make sure you are able to do the best possible job by practising your speech as much and as often as possible.

3.3 Breathing

This is very important: and I don't just mean to keep you from passing out!

A proper breathing technique is one of the most important weapons in an effective public speaker's armoury, in that it can:

> • Help you to relax.

> • Provide much-needed oxygen to the brain, in turn boosting your performance, helping you to think clearly and calming you down.

> • Help in your projection.

> • Stop you from rushing through the speech and provide you with a way of pacing yourself that not only sounds natural but feels it too.

The biggest danger when you're waiting to start speaking is that you panic, which can lead to you making fast, shallow, out-of-control breaths: otherwise known as hyperventilating. Hyperventilation starves your brain of oxygen, hindering your thought processes, and in turn making you panic as you realise you can't remember your opening line.

Most of us already think we know how to breathe properly: after all, we've been doing it all our lives without really thinking about it, right? However, certain ways of breathing are more effective than others, particularly for the purposes of public speaking.

Exercise 2 – Breathing through the diaphragm

The following technique is used by actors, singers, musicians and professional public speakers to ensure that they don't run out of breath at just the wrong moment.

• Take your left hand and rest it on the centre of your chest, on top of your breastbone.

• Place your right hand over your stomach, just above your belly button.

• Now breathe normally. You'll no doubt notice that your left hand moves in and out in time with your breathing, while your right remains still. This is how most of us breathe in our day-to-day lives; however, it's not the most efficient way if you want to get your voice across to a large group of people or over a long distance.

• Keeping your hands in the same places, imagine instead that you are trying to breathe through your stomach, so that your right hand moves in and out while the left stays still.

• Try this a few times, breathing as deeply, as slowly and as regularly as possible. You should notice that you are able to take much more air into your lungs than when you breathed before. Keep breathing, counting in your head as you do so: in – One. Two. Three. Four. As far as you can comfortably go. Then hold it for a second, and breathe out – One. Two. Three. Four. Until it feels like you've emptied your lungs.

• This is known as "breathing through your diaphragm": the diaphragm being the muscle at the bottom of your lungs which pushes the air in and out as you breathe (and the thing that vibrates when you have hiccups).

After breathing like this for a little while, you'll notice a few things happening:

• You're not hyperventilating, but instead are breathing in a calm, measured manner.

• You have so much more air available to you as you breathe out: this will help when we come to look at projecting your voice, in chapter 12.

• The extra oxygen getting to your brain makes you feel alert and focused, more aware of what's going on around you.

• You're focusing on your breathing and not on anything else that's bothering you: another thing helping to protect you against panic!

Once you get the hang of this technique you should practise it whenever you can: whether you're standing in a queue, walking down the street, or just sitting and watching TV. You'll notice it's not that hard and most of us have done it at some point in our lives without realising. As with most things, the more you practise, the easier it gets. This is something you can practise in public without getting too many strange looks.

In terms of when to use this technique, I'm not suggesting you do this all the time. However, there are certain points when you should use it:

• When you're sat waiting to start speaking and feel yourself beginning to panic.

• Just before you start to speak: while you're being introduced or waiting for the applause to die down.

• At handy breaks in your speech: such as when you change over a prompt card (see chapter 11 on using prompt cards and chapter 12 on timing).

• Breathing is also a great way of breaking up and pacing your delivery: it's a good idea to mark out in your speaker notes when to pause and take a deep breath, just as a reminder in case you forget (it can happen very easily!).

Otherwise, let yourself focus on the other stuff, like remembering what to say and how to say it. If you find yourself starting to panic, struggling for words, or just at a loss for something to do, then remember to breathe.

As mentioned above, one of the useful side-effects of breathing in this way is that it fills your lungs with more air, which then helps you project your voice. We're going to look at projection more in chapter 12 below.

3.4 Visualisation and Positive Mental Attitude

So, nerves are just your body trying to help you. Used in the right way, nerves can:

> • Give you the energy to deliver a knock-out performance.

> • Give you the incentive to prepare properly (and therefore avoid the reason why 99% of speeches fall flat).

> • Show you and others that you really do care about this speech and what you're talking about.

However, if you let them run unchecked then they can get in the way of your performance and enjoyment of the day. In this section we are going to learn a very simple, but extremely effective, way of dealing with nerves and using them to help you prepare for your speech. It's called visualisation.

Visualisation is just putting yourself in the best possible frame of mind so your nerves don't hinder – and in fact can help – you as you get ready to stand up and make your speech. We'll cover two different ways of doing this: using visualisation to help calm your nerves, and using visualisation to help you achieve a positive result.

Visualisation to calm your nerves

Visualisation can be a very effective relaxation technique which, used along with the breathing techniques above, can help you ensure that your nerves don't get the better of you.

Exercise 3 – Step by step visualisation technique

The following exercise provides an introduction to how visualisation can get you in a calm and comfortable state of mind. The key thing is to practise these techniques little and often: as with anything, plenty of regular practise is the key to getting it engrained in your memory and making it work for you

Find yourself a nice quiet place with no distractions. To make this work best, you'll need to close your eyes and relax, so you may find it helps to have someone to read this to you.

• Focus on your breathing. Breathe in deeply and count to four as you do so. Then exhale slowly, counting to four again.

• As you breathe in, imagine yourself drawing in pure clear air; and then expelling all the impurities from your body each time you breathe out.

• Feel yourself relaxing from your toes all the way up your body to the top of your head. Focus on each part of your body becoming more and more relaxed: first your toes, then your feet, then up your legs to your knees. Then your thighs and up to your stomach. Feel the relaxing sensation spread through your chest and down your arms, all the way to the tips of your fingers. Then feel the relaxation spread up your neck and into your head. Finally, let the sensation spread to your forehead, your eyes and eyebrows relaxing.

• Now imagine yourself walking slowly down a staircase. With each step you get more and more relaxed, until you reach the bottom and you're totally relaxed.

• Now picture a door at the bottom of the stairs. Open it and step through.

• You find yourself in the most relaxing place you can imagine. It could be somewhere you've been on holiday, or somewhere from your childhood, or even just somewhere you've seen in a magazine or on TV.

• Imagine how the place feels: for example, if it's sunny, feel the heat on your skin.

• Imagine the sounds and smells of the place, until you feel like you are really there.

• Dwell there, letting nothing else intrude.

• Focus on how you feel: how relaxed you feel. Latch onto that feeling.

• In order to make this work for you any time you need it, you need to anchor that feeling in your mind, give yourself a trigger which will take you back to this special, relaxing place whenever you want to. This should be something which you can do whenever you want to bring back that relaxing feeling. I would suggest you pinch your thumb and middle finger together. Do this while you're still in that relaxing place and focus on associating this gesture with the feeling.

• Take your time in that relaxing place, bringing yourself out slowly when you are ready to do so.

Practise this as many times as you can, until you are able to summon up that relaxing feeling at will, just by doing your trigger gesture.

Visualisation to achieve a positive result

We've already done this above, when you imagined how well everything would go. In my view, this is far and away the best method of conquering nerves. Sportspeople will often use this to help in their motivation and to get them mentally prepared to succeed. Here are some examples:

• The Jamaican sprinter Usain Bolt, after he set a new World Record at the 2009 Athletics World Championships, said: "I just visualised and then executed my plan".

• Megan Jendrick, the record-breaking American swimmer once said: "I have been visualising myself every night for the past four years standing on the podium having the gold medal placed around my neck".

• Immediately before they started playing their first European Championship final at Wembley, two of the FC Barcelona footballers visualised extremely vividly their success in the game to come, arguing about how many steps there were up to where the winners collected the trophy.

This may sound big-headed or strange, but it is an essential part of any successful sportsperson's preparation.

They imagine only positive outcomes: picturing themselves standing on the winner's podium, everybody cheering them, feeling the weight of that gold medal around their neck. Olympic athletes will spend years picturing this until it is as good as reality to them. In doing so, they make it that much likelier that they will work harder to achieve this outcome and succeed, and be ready for that success when it arrives.

Exercise 4 – Positive mental attitude visualisation

You can do this too. Close your eyes and imagine yourself having just finished your speech. Picture the room, the smiling faces, hear the laughter and applause, feel that warm glow of pride and satisfaction. Do it again and again.

By constantly picturing this positive scene, you are training your subconscious mind to expect this positive outcome. Our brains are amazing things and, by allowing yourself to imagine this, your brain can actually help to make it happen. By visualising a positive outcome you make it more likely that you will work harder to achieve that goal, and this will also help to block out those negative thoughts which create nerves and stop you doing the best you can.

It's only natural for a part of your brain to try and take over at this point, nagging you with thoughts of "what if everything goes wrong?". I'm not saying you should get rid of these thoughts altogether, as they're also a great incentive for you to prepare as well as possible. Just don't let them take over so you get paralysed by fear and negative thoughts. Remember: these bad things won't happen because you will be fully prepared.

3.5 Why alcohol is never the answer

There is often a tendency for people to have a glass or two of something strong to steady their nerves and give them a bit of "the old Dutch Courage". This is never a good idea:

> • Alcohol is a relaxant and so will actually calm you down too much. Remember, you need some nerves for the adrenaline it produces to help you focus and boost your performance.

> • Slurred words and losing your place can result from even a little bit of alcohol: particularly if you're worked up, tense and stressed to start with.

I'm not necessarily advocating complete abstinence: I've been to enough weddings to know how hard that can be. However, if you do drink, keep it to small amounts and save the heavy stuff for after you're finished speaking, safe in the knowledge of a job well done.

Reasons to Not be Fearful: Summary of main points

• Nerves can be a helpful, positive thing if you let them be.

• Identifying why you're nervous can really help in dispelling those fears.

• Everyone will be on your side, regardless of your role on the day.

• Deep, regular breathing through your diaphragm can work wonders in calming your nerves.

• Visualising positive outcomes can also be a big help.

• Don't fall into the trap of using alcohol to help you.

***

Chapter 4 - Logistics and Preparation

In order to succeed at anything – and this includes speech-making – you need to plan and be prepared. This chapter identifies what you need to have ready before you start thinking about what to write, let alone putting pen to paper (or finger to keyboard).

Let's start with three key questions: When, what and how?

4.1 When to start?

Many people flounder on this basic question: when is too early, or too late?

There's a short answer to this one. It's never too early to start.

Some people believe they work better under pressure, and so prefer to leave it all to the last minute.

This may be an exciting way to do things, but when it comes to making a speech it's also a sure-fire recipe for panic. Even worse, chances are you'll end up with something that's cobbled together (and comes across that way) and is therefore nowhere near as good enough as it could be.

This speech is important: not only to your audience / the happy couple / your daughter / future other half, but also to yourself. Otherwise why are you bothering to read this?

Make sure you give yourself enough time, and start planning your speech as soon as possible. As a rule of thumb, start at least two to three months before the day itself.

You should aim to have a finished speech at least three weeks, ideally a month, before the wedding. That way you'll have plenty of time to practise, review and get comfortable with it so that it's pretty much committed to memory by the time you have to stand up for real.

If you've not yet started and the wedding is sooner than this then start now: there's no time like the present.

Remember: if you're already nervous or worried about doing your speech, then putting off the preparation is just heaping yet more pressure on yourself. Why would you want to do this?

A word of warning.

Some people will tell you they didn't write their speech until the night before or even the morning of the wedding. Some may say they just made it up as they went along.

Don't listen to these people.

Admittedly, there is the odd genius who is able to do this and do it well, but they are extremely rare. If you know one then you should pick their brains now, as that sort of ability is like gold dust. Certainly I've never met one.

Nine times out of ten, these last-minute speech writers will either be:

(a) lying, or

(b) telling the truth but actually didn't do a very good job.

Even seasoned public speakers (like politicians or comedians) will spend days, weeks or even months planning what they will say and practising it over and over until they're happy with it.

Your aim is to do the best possible speech, not to win some sort of bravado contest. If appearing brave and talented is important to you, here's a tip. Still give yourself plenty of time to prepare, but then lie about when you started writing!

Exercise 5 – What do you need to prepare?

Before you start researching and pulling together your speech there are a few questions you should get answers to. Ask those in the know (organisers, bride and groom, their family, etc.) and make sure you fully understand the answers. A bit of time and effort here will pay dividends later.

    • What are you expected to say? Are you expected to do a full-blown speech or just say a few words?

    • Are there any time restrictions or an ideal length that the organisers would like you to stick to?

    • Is there anything the bride / groom particularly want you to include in your speech?

    • Alternatively, is there anything they'd really rather you didn't say?

    • When will you be expected to say it? What is the timing of the speeches?

    • What are the constraints of the venue? For instance, if there aren't any facilities for video or a slide show, then there's no point building your whole speech around it.

    • What are the other speechmakers going to say? You don't want to all say the same thing.

    • Who are your audience? What are the boundaries and what should you avoid saying? We cover this in more detail in chapter 5.

4.2 How should you prepare?

There are a couple of things which will make your preparation so much easier.

Notebook

Inspiration can come at different times for different people. For me, some of my best ideas come at awkward times such as when I'm walking, in the shower or even in the dead of night when I should be sleeping. To make sure I don't lose these ideas I've developed the habit of keeping a notebook with me at all times to scribble down my thoughts as they come to me.

I want you to do the same. Don't worry about grammar or keeping it neat: just make sure it's written in a way that you can read and understand later. If you jot down every thought as and when they come to you, I guarantee that within a few weeks you'll have more than enough ideas to be getting on with.

Make full use of your notebook. Every time you have an idea, no matter how small or seemingly obscure, write it down. Try setting yourself a target at the start of every day or week: for example, to come up with at least 10 ideas a week.

Having your notebook on you can be invaluable if you're down the pub and discussing the groom / bride with friends: if you're like me, over the years you'll have heard hundreds of great stories or jokes after a few drinks, only to forget them the next morning when you sober up.

Someone to critique your material

You should also make sure you have someone on hand who you can bounce ideas off, read your draft speech to and get an honest opinion from.

Many people resist this for a variety of reasons. Maybe they're afraid of being mocked or fear that their ideas aren't ready enough. However, having at least one other person on hand to sense check your material can be invaluable: after all, two heads are better than one. Another person could help you:

> • Think around a problem with the speech.

- Help pull you out of writer's block.

- Share the pressure by giving you someone to lean on.

- Help to calm your nerves.

- Give you a different perspective: give you useful feedback on what works and what doesn't.

This person should be:

- Someone who you can trust to give open, honest feedback that you will rely on.

- Someone who understands what you will be required to do and, more importantly, what the audience will be like.

- Someone you can trust to be objective. Avoid your other half, your parents or anyone who will be too supportive and not critical enough. You need someone who won't be afraid of hurting your feelings if what you're saying really isn't any good.

We often build up the worst possible idea of people's intentions, thinking they will try to sabotage your speech or make you look silly. This won't happen. However, if that's really your fear, make sure you pick someone you really trust.

You may think that, like a true artist, you don't want your masterpiece to be viewed until it is complete and perfect, or you don't want someone in the audience who knows your material. After all, won't this be one more person who won't laugh?

On the other hand, getting someone else involved will actually help you perfect your speech, for all the reasons I've mentioned above.

As for it ruining their enjoyment, don't worry. Your performance will change depending on a lot of factors, such as the audience's reactions, the adrenaline of the day itself and so on. In any case, that person will be supportive of you and will want you to do well. They will laugh in all the right places: indeed, they may even be the first to laugh as they know what's coming!

If you're still not convinced, then I have a very simple solution: choose someone who won't be there.

Logistics and Preparation: Summary of main points

• Don't leave it too late to start preparing your speech: the sooner the better.

• Make sure you have a full understanding of what is expected of you, what the logistics of the day are, and what the audience will be like (see also the following chapter).

• Keep a notebook to jot down ideas and stories as they come to you.

• Line up someone to help you prepare and practise your speech.

***

Chapter 5 - The Audience

Before you start writing it's important to consider who you will be talking to and make sure your speech works for that audience. This is arguably the single most important part of your wedding speech preparation.

Understanding your audience and moulding your speech accordingly helps:

> • Ensure you pitch it at the right level.

> • Ensure your jokes and stories are appropriate and less likely to fall flat.

> • Minimise the risk of getting the audience offside by offending them.

> • Ensure you don't bore or lose them by telling jokes they are never going to get (or find funny).

> • It can also help manage your nerves: all too often, we tend to imagine the audience as some huge monster which will eat us alive. By understanding who your audience is (and ensuring your speech is right for them) you can slay this demon and focus on just delivering your speech.

You can't please all the people all the time. You should though at least try to ensure you don't upset / offend the majority.

Exercise 6 – Understanding your audience

Get a copy of the guest list and understand who they all are. You may need to speak to the bride or groom or their parents to get this information.

Below are listed the key questions you should get answers to.

Make a note of the answers to these questions. Don't let it completely rule your preparation, but do cross-check back as you whittle down your material as well as when you've drafted your speech.

• What is the age profile of the audience? Will they all be young, or will there be a mix of ages present? (Different material will work better with an audience full of twenty-somethings than if there are people of a certain age present)

• Will there be families and children present? (In which case you'll need to tone down the "adult" material)

• What is their connection with the bride and groom or their families? (For instance, if they're from their church group, then the blasphemous material may need to be reconsidered...)

• Is the wedding to be a traditional or more relaxed one? Are you to be expected to do a very formal, traditional speech or do you have more freedom to experiment?

• Are there any sensitive subjects that you should avoid?

• Will there be any particularly argumentative or easily offended people there? (So you can try and avoid upsetting them, or be prepared to fend off any heckling with some well-prepared lines)

5.1 Understanding the boundaries

From the answers to the above you should have a good idea of the boundaries: what subjects are to be avoided and what level of joking is too far for your audience.

Remember: in assessing whether your speech works you should always judge it against your audience, not just what you (or your friends) consider to be funny. After all, it's not enough if it's just you laughing at your speech.

I find it helpful to keep in mind a person who is a mixture of the most conservative, easily offended people (or groups) in the audience: let's call them Aunt Maud and Uncle Alfred. Lump the worst qualities of your audience into these imaginary people – don't worry about turning them into a stereotype or cliché – and then imagine their reaction as you go through each line, joke and story. If they grumble only a little bit, then you're on the right lines.

The following are some things to avoid at all costs:

> • Anything generally considered in bad taste: such as racist or sexist material.

> • Contentious topics such as politics and religion should be treated with caution, and only used if you are 100% happy your audience will take them in the spirit in which they're intended.

> • The sexual history of the bride and / or groom should be avoided at any cost: their wedding day is really not the day for that sort of thing to come out.

> • Anything which will, or may, upset or embarrass the bride (see "The Wedding Effect" in chapter 2).

> • Poking fun at the family of the bride or groom is risky business, unless of course it's your own family and you know they'll take it well.

This is where it helps to have someone to help you and to critique your ideas. Use them to give you feedback on any ideas you have: are they appropriate or do you need to try something else?

The Audience: Summary of main points

• Understanding who your audience will be and moulding your speech accordingly is one of the most important aspects of your preparation.

• Get a good understanding of who will be there and whether there are any areas you really should avoid.

• Use someone else as a sounding board to ensure you stay on the right lines.

• Keep referring back to the information you gain here as you pull together your speech.

***

Chapter 6 - Getting Your Material

So now you're all set to start pulling together your speech: you have a pretty good idea of the expectations for your speech and who your audience are. How can you gather the material for your speech?

In this chapter we will discuss some of the various methods you can use to do this: not only sources of information, jokes and other material, but also what techniques you can use to get those creative juices flowing and end up with a truly original speech.

6.1 Research

Notebook

It's amazing the ideas and inspiration that can come to you at all times of the day. In the previous chapter I recommended that you keep a notebook to record ideas as they come to you, as well as to record any comments you may hear while you're talking to people, such as your mates down the pub. This will be your first port of call in terms of generating content for your speech, so if you've not already started using one then do so now: you won't regret it.

Friends and family

Talk to the friends and family of the couple. Once you know that you've got to write a speech, send an email round everyone asking them for at least one story each. Bribery is not necessarily a bad thing here: my best man started a competition with the prize of a bottle of champagne for the best story / photograph!

The internet

These days there is a wealth of information available, particularly on the internet. For example:

• Search engines. As a first port of call, try typing ideas or questions into an internet search engine and see what results come out. So, for example, if your groom's birthday is 12 April, put this date into Google (or Yahoo or Bing, or your other search engine of choice) and hit search. Among the results to come out include that he shares his birthday with the Spanish singer Montserrat Caballe (giving you something to say about his singing abilities maybe) and on this date the American Civil War started (maybe giving you a lead in to talk about his argumentative side). The following section on themes could also help here.

• Wikipedia. Sometimes wildly inaccurate, but then we're doing a wedding speech not a doctoral thesis. Never let the truth get in the way of an entertaining line (as long as it's not slanderous, of course..!). You can use this online encyclopaedia in much the same way as a search engine and it can often be a great source for other ideas: most articles will have a link to others which may take you to something of real use, so be creative. A word of warning: remember your goal and don't allow yourself to get too distracted.

• One-liners. There are a wealth of websites and books which provide lists of one-liners. My website www.perfectweddingspeech.com includes reviews of websites and books I have found useful, which I am updating all the time. Visitors to the site are also free to add their own, so this is a growing resource and worth a visit.

• Trade and specialist sites. If the bride or groom is interested in a specialist topic, such as a hobby or football team, then look around for websites dedicated to these subjects.

A word of warning:

Don't forget your overall objective, which is to generate some good ideas which can be included in your wedding speech, either as jokes, stories or overall themes. It can be easy to get distracted at this stage, particularly if you're using that great time-waster, the internet. Try to be as disciplined as possible, otherwise time will tick by and you'll still be no closer to having a speech you can use.

Other sources

Although the internet is a great source of information, don't forget other, more traditional sources, for example:

• School reports – if you can get hold of these then they can often be a goldmine of material for your speech. This is especially the case if they point out embarrassing childhood habits or make some comment which is even funnier in hindsight. For example, a dig through the groom's old school reports may tell you how he was always bad at maths, which could lead to a line in your speech like: "Steven never was very good at maths, which is of course why he is now such a successful bank manager…" Don't let the truth get in the way of a good joke here. If you don't have the actual reports, but do have a good idea of something which could have been said then there's no harm in making it up, as long as it's in good spirits and won't cause offence. As mentioned above, this is a speech not a thesis; a bit of "artistic licence" is perfectly fine, as long as it passes your key audience tests (see chapter 5).

• Encyclopaedia – you can use these in much the same way as Wikipedia above. Look up any topics which might be relevant to the person you're talking about (such as their birth place, favourite hobbies, recent holiday destination or any role models) and see what comes up. If you find anything interesting or amusing, then write it down in your notebook.

• Magazines and newspapers – keep an eye on the news for anything which even vaguely reminds you of the person you'll be talking about. This also applies for any past news that might be relevant. For example, if they're known for being clumsy and recently holidayed in a country where there was recently some sort of unrest or diplomatic incident, you could tie these together for comic effect.

6.2 Themes

Themes are something which we will be returning to in chapter 7, when we look at building and structuring your speech, but they can also help in your brainstorming (see the next section), providing you with some headings under which you can start to come up with ideas.

Below are some suggestions of themes which could help you build and organise material for your speech.

Exercise 7 – Themes

Here's your next exercise. Go through the following lists and jot down any thoughts which come to mind under each topic. Also try using some of the research sources mentioned in the previous section. If you're struggling with something to put under a particular heading, then ask around: someone's bound to have some nuggets of information which you can use.

About them (i.e. the person you're talking about: the bride if you're the father of the bride / groom; the groom if you're the best man)

> • Personality / character traits: are they clumsy or lazy or have a particular phobia?

> • Hobbies: do they have an unusual hobby or collect things?

> • Sport: teams or sports they support or play

> • Their family and friends: any unusual or amusing facts here?

> • Star signs

> • Films they like, or which bear a resemblance to their life

> • Characters / famous people they resemble or use as role models

> • Where they live

> • Family history: unusual relatives or surnames?

> • Music they like

> • Technology and other fetishes

> • Their pets

Their past

> • Where / when were they born?

> • Holidays they've been on

> • Memories from school and growing up

> • Key milestones: such as significant birthdays, passing exams, leaving home, learning to drive

- Growing up
- Events from life: e.g. stories from school, university, work.
- Cars they've had
- Their education and qualifications
- Jobs

Their future

- Their ambitions and plans for the future

Their relationship with their new "other half"

- How they / you met
- First date and initial reactions to each other.

The day itself

- The date of the wedding
- The church
- The venue for the wedding reception
- Any noteworthy guests

Other things relevant to the day and/or the happy couple

- Historical events (i.e. on this day in history…)
- Animals
- Adverts
- Locations

If there are a few themes from the above which generate ideas for you, then your speech is already taking shape! However, don't worry if you don't think you have as much as you need: if this is the case, try the brainstorming exercises below.

6.3 Brainstorming

Brainstorming is a great way to generate as many ideas as quickly as possible.

Exercise 8 – Brainstorming

Take a blank piece of paper and a pen. For this purpose, don't have anything else in front of you - just the paper. At the top of the page, write the following: "What could I possibly say about [insert name of your subject, be it the bride or groom]?"

Now take 5 minutes answering this question, writing down your ideas as a list. Don't think, just jot down the first things that come into your mind. I want you to be as creative and free thinking as possible, so don't worry about whether what you've written is factually right or acceptable or repetitive. The only rules are that you have to write down the first things which come into your head, without pausing.

Try to write down at least 20 possibilities, but when you reach 20, don't stop until you reach the end of the 5 minutes. If you get stuck at any point, ask yourself the following question: "What else?"

Ready? Good. Your 5 minutes start now.

Don't be afraid to try this as many times as possible, but make sure each time you limit yourself to just 5 minute bursts. That way, you encourage your brain to be as creative as possible.

The above question is deliberately vague, as everyone's individual circumstances are different. You may also wish to try different questions, either to make it more relevant to what you're trying to achieve, or to generate yet more answers. For instance, if the person you'll be speaking about is a bit of a practical joker, then you could ask something along the lines of: "What funny jokes has he pulled?" The important thing is to phrase these as questions with as many potential answers as possible, to help to stimulate the creative side of your brain. These types of questions are called "open questions" (such as "where would you like to go today?"), as opposed to "closed questions" which will typically have just a yes/no answer (for example, "do you want to go to the pub today?").

Don't worry if your list looks a bit bare: the best speeches are focused around just a few key ideas. If you really think that you don't have enough, take a break for a bit and then have another go, this time narrowing yourself down to some specific themes as headings for your brainstorming. See the previous section for some ideas here.

Keep adding to your lists as new ideas come to you. We will be using them very shortly but for now you have the beginnings of your perfect speech.

Mind maps

The above exercise used lists to set out your thoughts, but mind maps are also a very useful way of generating ideas quickly and easily. Particularly popular with free-thinking, creative types, these can also be very effective for those who are more structured in their thinking but find themselves obsessing over where in a particular list a certain point should sit.

A mind map is essentially a way of capturing thoughts and relationships in a manner which encourages you to be creative. Below is an example of one for those who haven't come across them before.

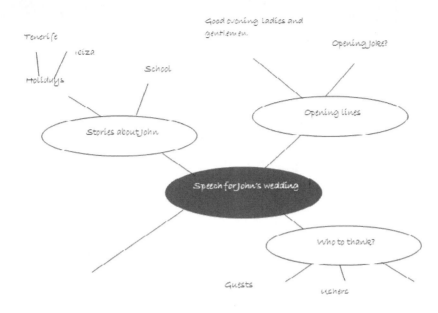

To start your map, set out your central question or subject in the centre. As a starter I'd suggest "Speech for [Name]'s wedding", but feel free to amend if you want. Then jot down anything you can think of which is even vaguely relevant as a secondary point: the next "spoke" out on the wheel. Don't worry too much about whether what you're writing down is suitable: the main aim is to just get things down and see where they take you. Anything relating to that secondary point can be written down as a subheader linked to the secondary point, and so on.

To create your mind map, use a large piece of paper: the larger the better, depending on how creative you're feeling!

Alternatively there are plenty of programs you could download to your PC or Mac: one I've used in the past is Freemind, which is free to download. For those of you with iPads, I fully recommend iThoughtsHD from the App Store, which does cost a small amount but is a really flexible and user-friendly mind mapping tool.

Research: Summary of main points

• The internet is a great source of information, but don't forget to also ask friends and family for their ideas as well.

• Also, don't forget your notebook!

• Themes can be used to order your thoughts, or to help generate new ones.

• Brainstorming and mind maps can be a very useful way of coming up with plenty of ideas – as long as you remember to be as free-thinking and creative as you can.

***

Chapter 7 - Structuring and Writing Your Speech

In this chapter we'll pull together all of the ideas you generated in the previous chapters into a first draft of your wedding speech.

7.1 Notes or a fully written speech?

A trap many people fall into is believing that they need to have a fully written speech in order to be able to speak in public. While it may be reassuring to have the whole speech written out word-for-word, this isn't actually necessary.

Why not? Let's think about what you'll be doing: talking and telling a story. These aren't new skills. In fact, these are the sort of things you'll have been doing since you first learned how to talk. The only difference is the setting and the number of people you'll be speaking to.

This isn't to say that you don't need to prepare at all. You still need to know what you're going to say. But don't get preoccupied with having an immaculate speech all laid out for you to read from, word for word. Notes and bullet points can be more than enough.

7.2 What is structure and why is it important?

One of the main reasons why a speech can seem to go on forever, even if it's a nice and short five minutes, is if there's no structure to it. The audience start by listening expectantly, but with no clue to show them where the speech is going they quickly become confused.

The problem is made worse if the speech rambles on over varying topics, with no clear common thread or theme. The audience stops listening as they come to the conclusion that even the speaker doesn't know where the speech is taking them. And if the speaker can't (or won't) make sense of the speech, then why should the audience?

Wedding speeches are no different to any other type of public speaking in that they need a clear and coherent structure, because:

> • It's easier for listeners to follow and understand.

> • It provides them with a frame of reference so they know how far through the speech you are.

> • It gives them confidence that you are fully in charge of your material, which in turn will make people respect you and want to listen.

> • It provides you with a framework that you can memorise and follow, giving you more confidence and enabling you to focus on getting your delivery right.

Structuring your speech is simply providing a framework within which the whole of the speech can sit, keeping it relevant and easy to follow. In turn this will keep people interested, stop you rambling and help you to remember what you are going to say.

7.3 The three sections of your speech

Breaking it down as simply as possible, your speech will have a beginning, middle and end. However, we shouldn't just stop there: each section itself should also be ordered in a sensible, logical way. The aim is to ensure that everything flows, so it's effectively just like telling a story to a group of friends.

Let's go through each of these sections in turn.

Beginning: introduction

The purpose of this section is not only to introduce yourself but also to show the audience what you'll be talking them through.

The beginning of the speech is where you are most vulnerable, but get it right and it can give you the confidence to get through the rest of the speech. There are a few things to remember here:

• Keep it simple. If there's one bit of your speech which you want to memorise word-for-word, the first few lines are it. Short, sweet and natural are the things to aim for.

• Introduce yourself: who are you? What is your relationship to the bride / groom?

• Opening joke: no pressure here, but first impressions count and if you can get people laughing straight away then you will get them on-side and also, just as important, give yourself a major confidence boost. Therefore, of all your lines, think carefully about this one. Try it out on a few people and make sure you are 100% convinced that it is a good one. Don't be afraid to use a corny or old joke: sometimes they can be the best as everyone will get the punchline straight away. Even a groan and a chuckle can be a good enough reaction: you're looking to engage people here, and to get them participating in / reacting to your speech.

• Thanks. Here's a little cheat which I've used successfully many times before (and also referred to in chapter 2 above). Start by thanking everyone: the parents for paying for the day, the couple for organising it, the bride for looking beautiful… This has a number of benefits:

- It makes you sound grateful and an all-round nice person, getting the audience on your side.

- It doesn't require too much in the way of creative thinking or preparation, although you do need to make sure you don't miss anyone important out!

- Applause means that people are paying attention, and it creates a great bit of peer pressure: everyone in the room will feel obliged to listen to what you're saying and respond accordingly. This is great if you're worried about having to drown out people still talking about the previous speech.

- By the time you've finished thanking everyone you'll be well into your speech, won't have used any gags yet and people will have not only formed a good impression of you, but would also have been clapping while you've been standing. You feel good, they've got involved, and now you're rolling! Try it: I guarantee it will work.

• Tell them in a couple of lines what they can expect. This will give a context to your speech, and show the audience that you have thought through how this will work. This is called "signposting", and we go through this in more detail in section 7.5.

Middle

This brings us to the middle, and the main part of your speech. As a rough guide this part should take up around 70% of the total time you're talking, with the other 30% split between your opener and the ending.

Here you will talk about your main stories, peppered with the odd joke. So first you need to take that long list of ideas which you brainstormed in the previous sections and whittle them down. Your aim here is to narrow down all your material (stories, jokes, anecdotes, etc.) into the handful (between three to nine as a guide) which you will use in your speech. The rest of this chapter gives you some techniques to achieve this.

End

Here you tie together your speech, repeating any key points you want people to remember, such as how much you love the bride (if you're the groom or father of the bride: it's generally not considered good form for the best man to do this…!), or how good a friend the groom is to you (if you're the best man). Traditionally people will end with some form of toast and then introduce the next speech: although if you have a toastmaster or compere then you may not need to do these last items. The golden rule is to check what's expected in advance, so you're well prepared.

7.4 Sample speech outlines

The following are intended to help get you started, with examples of points you can include for each of the main types of speech. You can use these as a checklist to help you in planning your speech, and feel free to add or remove as much as you want: I often find that the hardest part is starting so hopefully this does that part for you.

Father (or mother) of the bride's speech

Beginning:

> • Introduce yourself and in particular your role (in case there are some who still don't know!).

> • Thank everyone for coming.

• Thank those who helped / contributed to the day.

• Signpost the rest of the speech (see the following section).

Middle:

• Provide an insight into your daughter's personality: what are her best qualities and also her more challenging ones? Be careful here: don't say anything she wouldn't be happy for the audience to hear.

• Amusing or interesting stories from when she was growing up.

• What she means to you.

• Talk about how proud you are of her: including praising how she looks right now.

• Talk about your new son-in-law: your first impressions of him, how he's fitted in to the family and how much he means to your daughter.

End:

• Thank people: to the extent you've not done so already, do it now!

• Tie together what you've said and summarise your key points, bringing it all back to the point and purpose of the day. For completeness, use signposting to sandwich the speech material (see the next section).

• Introduce the next speaker.

• End on a nice note: some kind words about the bride and groom are always a safe bet.

• Make a toast.

Groom's speech

Beginning:

• Introduce yourself and in particular your role (in case there are some who still don't know!).

• Respond to the father of the bride's speech: thank him for his (hopefully!) kind words.

- Thank everyone for coming.

- Thank everyone for their gifts.

- Thank those who helped / contributed to the day.

- Signpost the rest of the speech (see the following section).

Middle:

- How you met your new wife.

- How you proposed to her.

- Any interesting or amusing snapshots into your life together.

- Why you are still together / getting married.

- Be self-deprecating: acknowledge your flaws.

- Praise your bride: particularly how she looks today.

End:

- Thank people: to the extent you've not done so already, do it now!

- Tie together what you've said and summarise your key points, bringing it all back to the point and purpose of the day. For completeness, use signposting to sandwich the speech material (see the next section).

- Introduce the next speaker.

- End on a nice note: some kind words about the bride are always a safe bet.

- Make a toast.

Best man's speech

Beginning:

- Introduce yourself and in particular your role (in case there are some who still don't know!).

- Respond to the previous speeches.

- Thank everyone for coming.

- Signpost the rest of the speech (see the following section).

Middle:

- How you know the groom.

- Provide an insight into his personality: good and bad points.

- Embarrassing stories from his past: maybe from childhood, growing up or recent past.

- His achievements.

- His hobbies and interests.

- When you first met the bride: first impressions.

- What the bride means to the groom.

- Don't forget to complement the bride's appearance!

- Has being with the bride changed him?

- What the groom means to you as a friend.

End:

- Read out any messages from absent friends.

- Thank people: to the extent you've not done so already, do it now!

- Tie together what you've said and summarise your key points, bringing it all back to the point and purpose of the day. For completeness, use signposting to sandwich the speech material (see the next section).

- Introduce the rest of the evening's entertainment.

- End on a nice note: some kind words about the bride and groom are always a safe bet.

- Make a toast.

Bridesmaid / Maid of honour's speech

Beginning:

- Introduce yourself and in particular your role (in case there are some who still don't know!).

- Respond to the previous speeches.

• Thank everyone for coming.

• Signpost the rest of the speech (see the following section).

Middle:

• How you know the bride.

• Provide an insight into her personality. For instance, her good and bad points, including any suitable / interesting / amusing stories from her past: maybe from childhood, growing up or recent past.

• Her achievements.

• Her hobbies and interests.

• When you first met the groom: first impressions.

• What the groom means to the bride.

• Don't forget to complement the bride's appearance!

• Has being with the groom changed her?

• What the bride means to you as a friend.

End:

• Read out any messages from absent friends.

• Thank people: to the extent you've not done so already, do it now!

• Tie together what you've said and summarise your key points, bringing it all back to the point and purpose of the day. For completeness, use signposting to sandwich the speech material (see the next section).

• Introduce the rest of the evening's entertainment.

• End on a nice note: some kind words about the bride and groom are always a safe bet.

• Make a toast.

7.5 Key techniques to use

Telling a story

Rather than getting worried about a lack of speech-writing experience, or stressing over the right form of words to use, the process can be made a lot simpler if you think of it as just telling a story: like you would to a group of friends.

Building your speech in this way has a number of benefits:

- We've all told stories to friends or family before, even if it's the story about what we did that morning, or what happened on a particularly eventful night out. You may not realise it, but you already have the skills needed for this, and to do it well. Story telling is one of the first skills we learn as children.

- Stories, especially those which follow an interesting and logical order, are easier to memorise.

- They are easier for you to talk about in an animated and interesting way, so you will naturally come across as someone who people will want to listen to. Especially if you're talking about things you've experienced or people you know

- It makes the speech itself more interesting to listen to.

So how do you do this? As noted above, you already have these skills. A good technique is to just say it aloud as though you were talking to a friend, and record yourself doing it. Write it down, cut out the dull, repetitive bits that always slip in, and you have a first draft of your speech. Simple!

If this sounds simple, that's because it is: people are sometimes too keen to overcomplicate things, especially when it comes to speech writing.

Signposting

"Signposting" is basically introducing your audience to what you are planning to say in the rest of your speech and is an important part of any well-written speech.

Many people instinctively don't like the idea of signposting, of telling people what to expect in advance. This is mainly because they worry that they'll lose the element of surprise and that if people know what they're going to be told then they'll either tune out the bits they think aren't interesting or relevant, or decide not to listen at all. This is not the case, however:

- Rather than spoiling things for your audience, signposting should be thought of as whetting their appetites: a hook to encourage them to keep on listening. Think along the lines of a headline in the newspaper: just enough to let people know the broad subject and to make them want to learn more.

- Contrary to what you might think, audiences really do want to know what's in store for them. Adults in particular can find it frustrating not having any idea at all what's coming next. People like to feel at least slightly in control; by giving them advance warning they will feel a bit of that.

- People tend to respect speakers who are fully prepared and in charge of their material. By signposting you are basically reassuring them that you know exactly what's coming next, have thought it all through and that there's no danger of you overrunning or boring them to death by rambling on for too long.

- Signposting can also be a useful cue for yourself. By setting out where you're going, you're reminding yourself what the order of your speech is, reducing the risk of you getting lost partway through. If you do get lost then you can always refer back to your signposts as a way of getting you back on track.

- Finally, if there are parts which you think people will decide to tune out for, then maybe you should take those parts out..?

Signposting is not telling them each individual detail at the start, as this is just another way of boring people. Keep it short and sweet: enough to whet their appetite. Something along the lines of the following will do:

"...Today I'm going to tell you a bit about Steve, our times growing up together and how he became the man he is today..."

If we're going to map out a typical wedding speech opener it could go something like this:

Opening Line ("Good evening ladies and gentlemen, my name's Mike and I'm your best man for the day...") → Opening Joke → Signpost ("...Today I'm going to tell you a bit about Steve, our times growing up together and how he became the man he is today...") → Introduce Start of Middle Section ("So I thought I'd start by telling you about the Steve I first met...")

The Rule of Three

Where possible, everything should be grouped into 3s. This is because the number 3 is an aesthetically pleasing one and is also the most effective when it comes to lists. If in conversation someone is told a list of two items, they will tend to feel that it is incomplete and will typically wait to see whether a third item is coming.

There are plenty of memorable examples here:

- "Friends, Romans, Countrymen: lend me your ears..."
- "My lords, ladies and gentlemen"
- "The Good, The Bad and The Ugly"

To name just three...

The more observant among you may have noticed that I've used this already in our example opener above – look back to the signposting: "...Today I'm going to tell you (1) a bit about Steve, (2) our times growing up together and (3) how he became the man he is today..." There would be nothing wrong with just saying "I'm going to tell you a bit about Steve" or "I'm going to tell you a bit about Steve and how he became the man he is today", but using three points here makes it sound neater, nicer and more complete.

Themes

Chapter 6 introduced the idea of using themes for your speech. Themes are a common thread (or threads) which people can easily follow, adding to the feeling of you telling a story and keeping them engaged. Think of them as the headlines for your speech, headings under which you can group one or more ideas, stories or jokes. They also have the benefit of ensuring your speech doesn't come across as unstructured and rambling.

So what are the themes for your speech? You could say that the main theme is the occasion of the wedding, and that's certainly true. It's possible to build an entire speech around this one theme, talking about the institution of marriage: what it means to you, how you feel about the happy couple and what you wish for them for the future. Indeed, if you listen to any sermon in a wedding ceremony you'll find this theme used.

However, chances are that you'll need or want a bit more than this to make your speech feel complete and worthwhile. You should use the themes that you used as the basis for brainstorming in chapter 6, including the other ideas you've come up with (from your research and that notebook you've been carrying around with you). Out of all these you should have a good list of themes, some of which will also hopefully have a good list of ideas under them.

In the next section we're going to look at how to whittle down this long list of ideas into a much shorter and more manageable list, which we will then start forming into your speech.

7.6 How to whittle down your ideas

Exercise 9 – Cutting down your ideas

To start with, take all the output from your brainstorming and research. On a blank sheet of paper, set out a list of the headings, being key themes which you'd really like to talk about or the ones which feel the most promising.

Now put each of your individual ideas under the heading or headings which best apply to them. Some will be straightforward, some may fit under more than one heading, and others may need a new heading. Don't agonise too much about this: just try and arrange everything as best you can. Do this with all your ideas, trying to group them together as much as possible. You may find that new ideas or themes come to you as you go along: if so, jot these down also. We're aiming for as many thoughts as possible.

Once you have completed this, cut out any headings / themes which:

> • Have the least number of points under them (unless there's a really good one there).

> • Are the least relevant to what you want to say (or to the other headings on your list).

• Are actually unsuitable to the occasion or the audience – such as controversial topics, or those which are downright offensive – see chapter 5 for more on this, as well as below.

• You don't feel comfortable or happy with. Allow yourself to be guided by your feelings here.

Similarly, highlight those which you absolutely think are winners.

Now pick up a red pen and imagine yourself as the worst possible member of your audience (Aunt Maud and Uncle Alfred from chapter 5). Put a line through anything which that person will hate. Be ruthless. I'll give you a hand to start with: anything involving the following should be struck out straight away unless you can give me a really, really good reason why not:

• Previous conquests: probably not the most tactful subject to bring up on a wedding day, especially in front of the new in-laws… A possible exception here would be if you're talking about when he/she was, say, five years old – as long as it doesn't risk making the bride or groom jealous, of course.

• Illegal behaviour: you and your mates may laugh about the night when the groom spent a night in the cells for exposing himself when drunk, but there's a pretty good chance that the bride's parents will not. Speaking of which…

• Drunken behaviour: this could work if you phrase it right, but be very careful that you stay on the right side of taste and humour, bearing in mind your audience. I once endured a speech which went into great detail about the groom's many episodes of vomiting after having drunk one too many. They went down great with his friends (20 of them) but not so great with the family and other guests (100 of them - most trying to work their way through dessert… you get the picture!).

• Anything which belittles / upsets the bride: you may need to do some research here by asking around those who know her and make sure you know exactly how far to go with your jokes. If in doubt, play it safe. I can guarantee that the quickest and easiest way to lose your audience and "die the death" (as comedians call it) is to upset the bride. It's her day (no matter what you may really think about her): remember this and you'll be fine.

• Ditto for family of bride / groom: you may be able to get away with this if it's your own family and you know they won't take offence, but I'd strongly advise against poking fun at someone else's family. Weddings are emotional enough without an all-out brawl between the new in-laws, believe me!

• In-jokes: the best way to exclude a large part of your audience is to use in-jokes which they don't – or can't – understand. Avoid these unless you can explain them in a simple and effective way that everyone will understand and, most importantly, find funny.

• Religion: this is one thing that many people feel extremely strongly about and so you should steer clear of any jokes or comments which may cause offence on the grounds of religion.

• Race: same applies here as it does for religion. Just don't do it and you'll avoid a pitfall from which you will really struggle to recover (and probably won't recover at all).

• Politics and sexism are also things you should steer clear of if you are in any doubt.

If you're having trouble whittling your selections down, then enlist help from someone who can provide a critical, independent view. Importantly, this person won't be as wedded to that amazing idea which you feel that you just have to keep because it's so funny: unless it really is funny. Do listen to other peoples' opinions: often something which seems hilarious in the thinking loses something in the telling.

Going back to the Rule of Three, try to aim for a maximum of three themes with three subtopics underneath them: you may need to be ruthless here.

After all this, hopefully you've still got plenty to work on. Don't worry if it looks like you've not got much left: to fill a decent sized speech you'll need no more than a handful of items. After all, you're only aiming to speak for five minutes. This may sound a lot, but it isn't in reality.

If you're really struggling, go back to the brainstorming exercises in chapter 6, or ask around for ideas. Also, think about the items you crossed out or didn't use at the start of this exercise. Is there a different spin you could put on any of them to make them acceptable?

Remember that you're aiming to be speaking for no more than 5 minutes, so 2 sides of typed A4 paper will be more than enough.

Now you should have a list of items which you would feel comfortable using. Take a highlighter pen and highlight your absolute best ones, limiting yourself to no more than 9. Be ruthless and again don't be afraid to ask for advice or assistance here. Good luck!

7.7 Actually writing the speech

Now comes the time consuming part – getting it down on paper.

Here are some things to bear in mind:

> • Keep it as natural as you can: write it down as you would say it.

> • Don't feel that you have to use perfect grammar and get it right word-for-word: especially not your first draft. The editing stage (see the following chapter) is where you can cut out any errors or bits you don't like.

> • As you'll see when we discuss the different ways of preparing your speech notes (chapter 11), notes and bullet points are perfectly fine for these purposes. The main thing is that you get the main points down in a format which you can follow, use and (most importantly) read.

> • Limit yourself to just one thought, story or point per paragraph (or bullet point). This makes it easier for you to read back over, as well as review it and rework it later on (see the next chapter.

> • Remember to try and tell a story as you write: you should find this also helps get your thoughts down on paper.

How to deal with the dreaded Writers' Block

Writers' Block is the name given to that horrible moment when people find themselves unable to write; when as hard as they try they just can't come up with the words to put down on paper. It can happen to any of us, and often at the one moment when you really want – or need – to be writing. It's almost as though someone is sitting in your head with a big eraser, scrubbing out every thought before you can get it down.

Often it's just a case of not knowing how to start. Other times it can be more the case of not having enough ideas, or not knowing which ones to use first.

In terms of starting, the only thing you can really do is force yourself to do it. Don't waste time agonising about the perfect opening line: if you're struggling with your introduction then put it to one side and start further in to your speech, somewhere where you already have plenty of ideas ready. You'll find that once you get started, regardless of where that is, the rest will come a lot easier.

If you've followed the stages in this book so far then you should have more than enough ideas to fill your speech. If you feel like you need some more, then have another go at the brainstorming exercises in chapter 6. Remember to also speak to others to get their ideas: it's amazing how this can give you a completely different perspective on things and start new ideas flowing.

In terms of getting your speech down on paper, a useful way to start is to set out your thoughts or key ideas as sub-headings on a piece of paper, then flesh them out or explain them below those headings. Once you are finished, you should be able to just remove the sub-headings and – hey presto! – there's the first draft of your speech. Don't get stuck agonising over the order at this point: the editing stage is where you try to perfect it all. For the moment you just want to get it all down on paper.

Structuring and Writing Your Speech: Summary of main points

- A good structure can make the difference between a speech being excellent, or just plain boring.

- Think of your speech as telling a story to your friends or family.

- Signposting can help keep your speech interesting and relevant.

- Group things into threes wherever possible for maximum impact and ease of listening.

- Use themes to order your speech and whittle down your ideas.

***

Chapter 8 - Editing

First of all, take some time out. Give yourself a week or so of not looking at your speech.

This way you ensure that, when you pick it up again, you'll have fresh eyes and can read it without being too precious about editing it. This is one of the reasons why you should give yourself plenty of time to prepare.

Exercise 10 – Editing your draft speech

Once enough time's gone by, take your first draft and a red pen and read your speech with an extremely critical eye. Be ruthless here: think about your audience and amend, edit, strike out. You may find it easier to read your speech aloud: either to yourself or to others. Think about the following:

 • How does it flow? Does it make sense? Would it be better in a different order? Try to get it so it's like listening to a story. To help here, you can use signposting (see chapter 7) as a way of helping the flow of your speech. For example: "Enough about his schooldays, now let's say a few words about his working life…"

 • Are there any over-complicated words or sentences? Remember that you'll be saying this out loud, so avoid any words which you wouldn't usually use, or have trouble pronouncing. Use a thesaurus to find better words if you're stuck. Practising reading your speech aloud can really help here. If you stumble when reading a word or sentence aloud for the third or fourth time, then delete it.

 • Does it move quickly enough? Bear in mind that you should have just one paragraph for each thought / story, so any paragraphs which are longer than a quarter of a page may need reworking and cutting down. Think about your audience: are they likely to be bored? If you're bored reading it, then you definitely need to rewrite it.

• Length: as I said before, the ideal length should be around five minutes and definitely no longer than ten minutes. In long form (i.e. not notes), a typed sheet of A4 will average about two to five minutes in length when read aloud, so with that in mind you should have no more than two to three pages of A4. Read your speech aloud and time it, remembering to add a bit extra for applause, laughter, etc.

• Unsuitable material: constantly ask yourself whether your speech is suitable. Will it cause offence? Will it be funny? Imagine the worst possible member of your audience: the most conservative person ever. Now imagine their reaction. If they're not too upset, you're on the right track.

Don't be disheartened if you find that you have to rewrite it all: this is very common. I'll usually go through at least two or three rewrites until I get something I'm happy with, and will keep amending almost every time I look at it. This is yet another reason why you should give yourself as much time as possible for this process!

***

Chapter 9 - The Importance of Practise

Finally, make sure you practise, practise and practise some more. You should do this by reading it aloud, rather than in your head: this helps you to identify any clumsy sounding words or sections. Remember, the whole purpose of your speech is to be read aloud, not to be seen on the page, so the most amazingly flowery language is useless if it doesn't sound right when spoken aloud.

Treat this as not just a way of learning your speech but also an extension of the editing process: don't be afraid to continue tweaking your speech as you go. By the time you come to actually making the speech, you should almost be sick of saying your speech and therefore pretty much have it off-by-heart.

I really can't stress this enough.

Make sure you make time each day to practise your speech. It doesn't need to take hours: just five minutes or so when you're driving in your car or walking to work.

Don't worry about getting it totally word-perfect each time. It may be that you come across a new way of saying or ordering it which works even better: if so, note it down and use it going forward.

Your mistakes can also sometimes be more helpful than the bits you can do word perfect: your mistakes may highlight something you need to spend more time on, or maybe show up a passage which is too complicated and needs to be reworded or cut out completely.

Little and often is definitely the key here. In this way you ensure that your speech really gets lodged in your memory: you should be well and truly sick of it by the time the big day comes!

You should also practise reading your speech to other people so that you can get their opinion on it, as well as get used to speaking in front of others. Key things to ask them include:

• Is your pace OK or are you speaking too fast or too slow?

• How is your projection? Would they be able to hear you at the back of the room you will be speaking in?

• Does the speech flow and make sense?

• Do the jokes work and are they appropriate?

• At what points should you pause?

• Is there anything missing which should be included?

• Is the length right or do you need to trim it?

***

Chapter 10 - Practicalities of the Day

Before we start, it's worth thinking about what else you'll need to do leading up to the day as well as the day itself. If nothing else, it's important to keep things in perspective – the speeches are only one (tiny) part of the overall occasion.

10.1 Your role

Typically your role on the day of the wedding will depend on whether you are involved in organising it, have been asked to help out, or are just turning up as a guest and speaking. The occasion and the people involved will also have a bearing, but below are a few pointers as to what to expect from a traditional, Western wedding:

The Groom's role

• Aside from getting married, you are one of the key hosts of the day, so ensure you speak to and welcome as many of the guests as possible.

• Ensure that the best man and the ushers know their roles.

• Liaise with the master of ceremonies (if you have one) to understand timings, what needs to happen and when, etc.

• Make your bride feel like the day is going smoothly.

• Be the first point of contact if there are any questions or issues.

The Father of the Bride's role

• You are another one of the key hosts of the day: you should welcome the guests and ensure they have all they need.

• Ensure your daughter is happy and enjoys the day.

• Be especially welcoming to the groom's family and friends.

• Give away your daughter.

• Welcome the groom to your family.

The Best Man's role

• Take the pressure off the groom where possible: support and assist him so he can focus on enjoying the day.

• Organise and oversee the ushers.

• Help to organise people for the photographs and other parts of the day, making sure everyone is in the right place at the right time.

The Maid of Honour / Head Bridesmaid's role

• Support and assist the bride, making sure everything is going as she would like it to.

• Organise the bridesmaids.

• Take as much pressure off the bride as possible, allowing her to enjoy the day.

The Bride's role

• Support the groom, especially if he's nervous about making his speech.

• Enjoy the day: let the others worry about whether everything's going as planned.

The Mother of the Bride's role

• As another key host of the day, ensure you're welcoming to the guests.

• Support your daughter, making sure everything's going as planned.

• Support your husband, especially if he's nervous about making his speech.

10.2 Checklists

Regardless of your role, below are a few checklists to help you remember what you need to do as you approach the day.

Before the day

• Speech written in plenty of time to enable you to practise.

• Practise your speech regularly: at least once a day.

• Any props required? If so make sure you have everything and have tested them to make sure they all work as they should. There's more on this at chapter 13.

- What order are the speeches going to be in?

- What toast should you make at the end of your speech?

- Check what the other speechmakers are going to say to ensure you don't duplicate.

- The layout of the room: does everyone have a chance to see and hear the speakers?

- Get your speech written out in a format you are able to read easily: see chapter 11 for more on this.

- Did I mention practising your speech?

The night before

- Make sure you have a final copy of the speech with you – whether in note or prompt format – preferably with at least one back-up.

- Also, if you're using any props, make sure you have them all and they're fit for purpose (see chapter 13 below for more on using props).

- Try to relax, but don't drink too much.

- By all means continue to practise your speech, but draw a line at a certain time: don't look at it again after 6pm at the latest. If you keep looking at it throughout the evening, you may end up stressed and unable to sleep: not the best preparation!

- If there is a pre-wedding meet-up, make sure you meet as many people as possible: this will help to humanise them and remove some of the reasons for you to be nervous.

- Ignore any scare stories about wedding speeches gone wrong. They won't apply to you: you're well prepared and practised!

All through the day

- Try not to think about your speech: there are many more important things to focus on during the day, and spending time worrying about the speech will stop you playing a full part in the day and enjoying yourself.

• If at any point you find yourself getting nervous, use the breathing and visualisation techniques at chapter 3 to help you relax and rediscover a sense of perspective.

The morning of the day

• Check you have your copy of the speech.

• If you have time, there's no harm in having one final run through of your speech, although don't panic if you find something not working or you forget something: if you've practised enough then all your preparation will see you good in the end.

• Now focus on your other duties: get dressed in your wedding suit / have you got the rings? / organise the bridal party / check all is OK at the church and venue / greet the guests / ensure the groom or bride get to the church on time / etc... I told you there were plenty of other, more important things to worry about than just one little speech!

Before you speak

• Make sure you have a full glass of water in front of you.

• Check your notes/prompts and have them laid out in front of you ready to start (see chapter 11 for more on this).

• Read the first line and ensure it is at the front of your mind: standing up and starting to speak is far and away the hardest part so get that out of the way and you'll find that the rest just flows.

• Use visualisation (see chapter 3) to imagine the amazing, wonderful job you're about to do: look around at all the faces in front of you and picture them all laughing and applauding you.

• Take nice, slow, deep breaths (see chapter 3): notice how focused and alert that makes you feel.

• Don't worry if you're still nervous or a bit wired: all that energy is going to come in handy (again, see chapter 3).

• When it's your time to stand, make sure you smile, take a couple of deep breaths, and then begin.

When you've finished speaking

  • Relax and enjoy the rest of the evening!

10.3 A reminder of the importance of practise

As mentioned above, it's important to start to prepare as early as possible, to enable you to practise as much as possible. I really do believe that practise is vital.

As well as giving you an opportunity to polish and perfect your speech, regular practise also:

  • Helps to lodge your speech in your long-term memory, so there's less risk of you forgetting it.

  • Identifies any areas you may need to rehearse more thoroughly.

  • Reassures you that you're actually far more prepared than you may otherwise fear.

  • Removes some of the mysticism and fear around the whole thing: if you know the words and have had plenty of practise saying them, then you're over 75% of the way there!

Put aside some time every day to practise your speech. This need only be five minutes: little and often is far better than putting in a few hours just one or two days a week. The important thing is that you take the time to go through your speech. Here are some ideas:

  • Out loud to other people to check your projection and timing.

  • To yourself, maybe looking into a mirror, in the car as you're driving to work, or under your breath when you're out walking (ignore any odd looks you get!).

  • Just running through it in your head.

The more you familiarise yourself with your speech, the lower the risk that you'll forget it or lose your way on the day itself. And therefore the more likely you are to be more relaxed in the run-up to the day!

***

Chapter 11 - Your Notes: Prompt Cards v Written Speech

On the day itself you'll want to ensure that you have your notes with you – but what form should they take?

There are at least two schools of thought as to how you should use your speech notes. You could either have the speech in front of you, word for word, set out exactly as you would read it; or use prompt cards with just key words and phrases to remind you of what to say.

Written Speeches

11.1 Advantages and disadvantages of written speeches

"Written speeches" in this context means your speech written out word-for-word pretty much as you would say it. This is the most intuitive and familiar way of having your speech with you (although as we'll see, arguably not the most effective).

What are the advantages of written speeches?

> • Most people will have drafted their speech in this way, and so already have the notes they need, rather than having to put additional thought and effort into producing something new.

> • They are easier to produce and more familiar: as a result they can be an obvious aid for the inexperienced.

> • People often like written speeches because they allow them to know at a glance where they are and where they're going next.

What are the disadvantages of written speeches?

• If you rely too much on them you can kid yourself that you don't need to practise: after all, you already have it in front of you, so why waste time practicing?

• Reading something word-for-word can lead to your delivery being stunted as you focus on reading rather than actually being entertaining or engaging.

• We all write a lot more formally than we speak: reading a speech which has been written out in long form can therefore sound a lot less natural than your normal way of talking.

• When you read it, you're likely to spend too much time looking down and reading, rather than making eye contact with your audience.

• These can all combine to make your delivery boring and unnatural.

11.2 How to use written speeches

If you decide to use a written speech you'll want to ensure you make the most of the benefits of having a written speech, and minimise the downsides. Here are some tips to help you:

• Preparation is key. Make sure you're fully familiar with your speech, reading it through and practising it as many times as possible, so that you could almost read it word-for-word without looking at the page. This way you should be comfortable with the flow of it and run a greater chance of not losing your place. Ideally on the day you should only be using your notes as a reminder of what to say next, rather than something you need to read word-for-word.

• In your practise sessions you should read from the speech in exactly the same way as you will on the day: glance down occasionally but keep the majority of your eye contact for the room. In this way, you'll identify sections you're less comfortable with and where you may therefore need more prompts to help you (or more practise!).

• Help yourself to be able to read your speech: remember the circumstances you'll be talking in. You want to have your notes resting out of sight on the table: holding them right under your nose can be off-putting for the audience, as well as seriously damage your ability to deliver your speech as clearly and interestingly as possible. Use big type in a neat font that you can read comfortably from a table top while you're standing up.

• The text should be big and in a colour which is easy to pick out from the page without being too distracting – black on white is a good choice.

• Avoid using capitals, as these can be hard to read. Try it if you don't believe me – there's a reason why lower case letters have the shape they do: so we can easily identify them with a glance. Capital letters are all the same size and so take a bit more effort to pick out from the page.

• If there's a section or a word that's really important, or a useful reminder for you, then neatly underline or highlight it in a different colour. Don't overuse this: if every other sentence is underlined, then you might as well underline nothing.

• Make sure there's plenty of white space on the page: this is easier on the eye and less confusing (and allows you to make any last minute notes without cluttering things up too much). Leave at least two lines between each paragraph (and maybe also between each line).

• Each paragraph should be no more than four or five lines at most, and ideally much less. Put an extra line between paragraphs and make sure the margins are nice and wide to give you space to make any notes.

• Include prompts to yourself in the speech, such as turning to gesture at or talk to someone, pause or clap: no matter how silly this may look on the page. It's very easy to forget such things in the heat of the moment. This even extends to giving yourself a prompt to pause and take a breath / sip from your drink!

• Make sure these prompts are marked out so that you don't run the risk of reading them out: I'd suggest [putting them in square brackets], or a different colour.

• If you have more than one page of notes, make sure you number them. You don't want a stray gust of wind to undo all that good preparation.

• When you come to read your speech, don't panic if you miss a word or get muddled. Remember: you're the only one who knows what should be coming next, so no-one else is going to notice if you say things in the wrong order or miss out a bit. If you can skip back to the bit you missed without it sounding odd then do so. Otherwise, move on.

• Avoid holding loose sheets in your hands: if you're nervous or you're just prone to the shakes anyway, this can be very distracting.

Prompt Cards

11.3 What are prompt cards?

Prompt cards are cards which are small enough to hold in your hand and stiff enough to not flop around if held one-handed. A good rule of thumb is to use one thought / story per card.

The intention is that they are used as prompts to remind you what to say next and where the speech is going, rather than setting the whole thing out word-for-word.

They should therefore include just enough to prompt you to remember what you'll be talking about. Let's take the example of an hilarious story about that skiing holiday in 2005 when the groom slid down a mountain face first and ended up with trousers full of snow. In long form this could read:

"…He's always been an elegant guy. I remember a ski trip a few years back where he was so keen to show us how great he was. On the first run of the day, we all assembled for a masterclass, only to watch him come down most of the mountain on his face; ending up with trousers so full of snow we weren't sure if it was him or the Michelin Man!"

Your prompt card for this could read:

Always elegant
Ski - Masterclass
First run -
On face -
Michelin Man!

11.4 Advantages and disadvantages of prompt cards

What are the advantages of prompt cards?

• There's less chance of you getting lost, or having those awkward pauses while you try and find out where you've got to in a long piece of text.

• They encourage you to be more natural, talking like you would in normal conversation (or when you're telling a joke) rather than a dull, monotonous reading voice.

• They help your projection and allow you to easily gain eye contact with the audience.

• They're easier to ad lib with: you may be planning to stick to the speech, but if something happens to break your flow (applause in a place you weren't expecting, a comment from someone in the audience), it's easier to recover with prompts than it is with a written speech.

• You don't need to worry about loose pages flapping around in the breeze or as your hand shakes.

• They give you something to do with your hands: if you really do need to hold onto something, then no-one will think it unusual if you're holding your cards, as long as you do so naturally, allowing your hands to move as you see fit.

• They look more impressive and professional!

What are the disadvantages of prompt cards?

• Unlike your written speech, which you'll probably already have, these require some extra work to turn them into a format you can use.

• They are unfamiliar and can be daunting to those who've never used them before.

• They require practise: reading from prompt cards doesn't necessarily come naturally.

Aren't prompt cards a bit too advanced?

In a word, no. At first glance using prompt cards can appear daunting or confusing: how will you know what to say? Does this mean you're going to have to memorise everything word for word?

There's nothing to worry about. Prompt cards are there to remind you where you are. In terms of memorising them, you should have a pretty good idea of your speech's flow from your practise runs. Don't try to memorise everything word for word. Allow yourself to ad lib to an extent, to tell the story as though you were talking to a small group of friends.

If a certain word or sentence is really important – for instance in a joke – then by all means write it down word-for-word. Otherwise don't be afraid to improvise and let things flow. This will help you to seem more natural and relaxed, creating a better impression in your audience's minds.

If you're going to use prompt cards, then you will need to incorporate this into your practise routine, so make sure that you pull together your prompts with plenty of time in advance.

11.5 How to convert your written speech into prompt cards

Start with a fully planned speech: either a collection of notes or bullet points or even a fully written speech, depending on your preferences and how far you have come in your preparations.

The first card is easy. Write out your opening paragraph in full. This is one of the few bits you'll include in this way, because:

> • Starting is always the hardest part, so having this in front of you takes away one potential worry.

> • If it's there for you to read, word-for-word, then you'll find it (and the following bits) that much easier to remember.

> • It can be extremely reassuring to have your first line there in front of you: it's often the beginning of the speech where stage fright can kick in.

Now move through your speech and divide it into sections. Each section should be a paragraph, a point or a series of related points, or a story.

Take a highlighter and pick out the minimum number of words you need to remind yourself what that section is about. This may be as little as one word, or a handful of words. Don't worry about forming a sentence: as long as it makes sense to you, that's the main thing.

Transfer your highlighted words to your prompt cards. Make sure there aren't too many words per card: you want to be able to use nice, big writing so that you can read it easily. If you find yourself trying to cram too much in, think about either cutting them down or splitting them onto more than one card.

Each card should consist of one self-contained point or story.

The main things to think about as you write your prompt cards are:

(a) does this make sense to me?

(b) does it prompt my memory? and

(c) can I read this and understand what it says at a glance, without having to peer too much at it?

If you've passed these tests, then you're on the right track.

Use only one side of each card. I know it's wasteful, but you want to minimise the risk of getting confused, and having to remember which side you've read just increases the risk of you getting into a muddle.

Number the cards as you go along: don't run the risk of dropping them and losing your order.

Use different colours to pick out key points or highlight stage directions, etc., but don't overdo this: you don't want to end up with a confusing mess of colours.

11.6 How to use prompt cards

As with notes, a key element of prompt cards is that you need to practise in advance: prompts are just a few words or sentences to remind you what to say. If you don't practise and prepare in advance, so that you are pretty familiar with what you're going to say, then you'll find yourself struggling on the day.

Ideally you want to be able to see two prompt cards at any one time: the one you're talking to and the one which is next in the running order. This means that you can move seamlessly from one to the other without the panic of wondering what you're going to say next. It also allows you to change pace or tone if your subject is going to change: upbeat if you're about to make a toast, downbeat if it's about absent friends.

It's very important that you clearly number the cards and keep them secured tightly together until you're due to speak – a bulldog clip is a good option here – don't rely on envelopes or keeping them loose in your pocket, as they may shuffle around if not held together.

In terms of reading the cards, you should only need to glance at them to remind yourself what to talk about: your endless hours of practise will fill in the rest. Allow yourself to relax and speak as naturally as possible. The beauty of prompt cards is that they free you from having to stick slavishly to a script.

If you find yourself struggling or losing your way, it's likely that nerves are getting to you. Take a deep breath, relax and try some of the techniques in chapter 3.

11.7 What if I'm not comfortable using prompt cards?

Then don't: you need to be happy and confident in what you're doing. However, I'd encourage you to give them a try.

Whatever method you use, I can't stress enough the value of practise. Practise, practise and practise and you'll be fine: don't try to learn if off-by-heart, but do keep practising until you automatically know what you are saying next, all the way through.

When I prepare to speak in public, I take every opportunity to practise: even when I'm walking down the street. I may get some funny looks, but by the time it comes to do it for real I'm fully prepared!

Finally, and most importantly, the speech is not something to ruin your time worrying about: so relax and enjoy yourself!

Your notes: prompt cards v written speech: Summary of main points

- Fully written notes can be a useful and easy way of having your speech with you on the day.

- Prompt cards take a bit more effort, but are much better at encouraging a more natural delivery.

- Make sure that your notes are easy to follow and read.

- Don't forget to practise!

***

Chapter 12 - Delivery

You could have the best, wittiest, most professionally crafted speech ever written, but if the audience can't actually hear you deliver it then you're just wasting your time. Likewise, the way you say something has a huge impact on how it is received: here's a little game for you. Take a guess at what percentage impact the following have on an audience:

- The words

- Your voice

- Your body language

The answer may surprise you. A study by Albert Mehrabian ("Silent Messages", 1981) found that the words only made less than 10% of the total amount of impact. Listeners paid more attention to, and were influenced more by, the way the speaker's voice sounded and, most important of all, the body language of the speaker. Body language on its own accounted for over 50% of the total influence on the listeners.

So you see, there's more to a successful speech than just having the words and reading them out!

It's not just what you say, but how you say it. In this chapter I'm going to teach you some simple techniques which can really transform the way you come across to the audience.

12.1 Breathing

This was covered in chapter 3, so I won't repeat myself here, except to remind you of how a proper breathing technique can help you to project your voice properly and clearly.

Deep, regular breaths from your diaphragm can not only help calm you, but also provide you with more air and lung capacity. This in turn can help to project your voice clearly and effectively, without the need to shout. So remember to take those nice, deep breaths: before you stand up and whenever you take a pause. They really will make a difference.

12.2 Projection

It may sound obvious, but one of the most important things about public speaking is being able to project your voice to all corners of the room. As I said before, you could have the finest written speech in the world but it's useless if no-one can hear you say the words.

This is where many people feel uncomfortable: our normal speaking voice often isn't loud enough for a large room of people. Shouting, on the other hand, is tiring, hard to listen to and maybe a bit rude. The good news is that just a few simple techniques can help you easily project your voice freely and clearly over large distances with little effort.

Exercise 11 – Projecting your voice

Find someone who can give you feedback on how your voice is coming across, as well as a space large enough to allow you to practise getting your voice across over a good distance. Ideally this would be similar to the room you'll be in on the day itself: if you can practise in the actual room you'll be speaking in on the day, so much the better.

• The first thing is to stand. It's traditional to do so in any case, to ensure that everyone can see who's speaking. This also allows you to make full use of your lungs: sitting compresses your lungs, while standing corrects this. Stand as tall and straight as you can, to allow as much air as possible into your lungs and back out again.

• Standing up also helps you to get the adrenaline flowing, and provides a nice small outlet for some of that nervous energy we talked about in chapter 3. But remember that you'll need most of that lovely energy channelled towards your voice!

• If you can't stand for whatever reason, make sure you have a good straight back with a posture that allows you to fill your lungs as much as possible.

• Next, you need to use the breathing technique we learnt in chapter 3. Take a deep breath in and out before you stand and then another one in just before you start speaking. Use these nice, deep out breaths to speak with. For this practise run it doesn't matter what you say, although this could be a useful opportunity to practise your speech...

• Using a deep "out" breath, speak in a slow, measured way, using all that breath for the first sentence. Imagine the air coming from your lungs, travelling up your throat and out of your mouth, carrying your voice with it. Don't let it out too quickly, or you'll run out of breath before you're ready to finish. Similarly you don't want to ration it too much, or you'll end up speaking too quietly. A bit of practise should help you to find the right balance which works for you. Don't forget to keep checking with someone (standing a good distance away) that you're sounding loud and clear enough.

• Then take another deep breath and do it again. Don't worry if you feel like you're sounding too slow: better this than gabbling through as it allows people more of an opportunity to understand what you're saying.

• All the way through, remember to stand straight with your hands and feet firm yet relaxed, breathe properly and keep eye contact with your audience. There's more on these important points below...

When practising, and on the day itself, it helps to have someone standing at the back of the room ready to signal if your voice becomes too quiet to hear (likewise if you're talking too quickly or too slow).

12.3 Posture

Next is posture: the way you should stand. When you speak your body uses all parts of your body to help project your voice: not just from the neck up. You should aim for a nice, straight back, with your shoulders back and your chest out: just imagine you're a kid again and playing at being soldiers. If you actually are (or have been) a soldier then you have an advantage: imagine you're on the parade ground in front of a particularly bossy Sergeant-Major!

You are aiming for a good, straight path for your voice to travel from your lungs all the way to your mouth.

This isn't to say you should stand ram-rod straight and uncomfortable all the way through your speech. As you start to get into your flow, allow yourself to relax into it and move as feels natural. You should though resist the urge to slump as this will just make you appear uncaring, not to mention doing nothing for your projection.

The next step is to think about how to hold your head. Effective speaking isn't just about getting sounds out of your throat; your mouth and the whole of your head (in fact, the whole of your body) play an important part in how well you project your voice.

Mouth open

You want to open your mouth as wide as possible when you speak: much more than you would normally feel comfortable doing.

Don't worry about looking weird or unnatural compared to how you usually speak. The rules change when you're speaking to audiences over larger distances. Think about actors in a theatre: to get their point across to the audience they not only speak louder but also exaggerate the way they speak and act.

Having a nice, wide open mouth when you speak has the following benefits:

> • It helps you project your voice.

> • It therefore helps the audience to understand what you're saying.

> • It also forces you to slow down your pace, therefore allowing people to follow you more easily.

Smiling

You should also focus on keeping a happy, welcoming expression on your face. Smile just before you start speaking (and if there are any natural breaks where people are applauding, etc.). This will:

> • Give you a nice, welcoming air which people are more likely to respond positively to.

> • Make your voice more positive and interesting.

> • Give people the impression that you are happy to be there and want to talk to them.

> • Release nice happy hormones into your system, helping you to (at least a bit!) enjoy the occasion.

> • Give people the impression that you are indeed happy and relaxed: and maybe even trick your body into feeling the same!

A word of caution here: make sure this doesn't appear too unnatural and don't overdo it. It's definitely worth practising this in front of a mirror and asking someone else to check how you're coming across.

Chin up

Keep your chin up while you're speaking, so that you're looking across the length of the room, rather than constantly down at your notes.

• A raised chin helps to stretch out your throat, giving the air more freedom to get out effectively.

• It also points your mouth in the right direction so you're speaking out at the audience rather than down to the floor.

• It helps you to maintain good eye contact with your audience (more on this below).

• Finally, it helps keep your delivery nice and measured.

The eyes

There's an old myth that, if you're nervous, you should look to the back of the room and avoid eye contact with the audience. I couldn't disagree more with this.

You should always make sure that you make eye contact with your audience:

• It raises your chin naturally, helping your projection.

• It makes you seem interested in your audience.

• It removes some of the fear you may have of the audience: rather than being some mass of horrible creatures from your imagination, by looking them in the eyes you help reassure yourself that they're human after all.

• It will get a positive reaction from them: even if it's just a little smile or nod.

• It encourages people to pay attention.

So, you should always seek to make eye contact.

But how and how much?

Here are some exercises to help you. You'll need some friends to help you here, but you don't necessarily need to set this up: these are exercises you can practise in normal conversation with a group of two or more other people, even without telling them you're doing it.

Exercise 12 – Eye contact practise 1

You need to make sure you hold your audience's eye contact for a good amount of time, but not too long that they feel uncomfortable.

How long? One thought or sentence is a good rule of thumb, up to a maximum of around five seconds. Any less than this feels unnatural and fake, any more can be off-putting and even embarrassing to the person you're effectively singling out for attention: not to mention the rest of the room, who'll start wondering why that person in particular deserves such special attention!

• Gather a group of two or more people together and ensure that you can see all of them.

• You don't necessarily need to practise your speech to them (although as mentioned before the more practise the better): these techniques are a great way to engage people in normal conversation as well.

• As you talk, make eye contact with one person.

• Hold eye contact for a maximum of 5 seconds, or one thought / sentence (if shorter). When you've finished, move on to the next person, holding eye contact with them for around the same amount of time before moving on.

• You'll probably find that you automatically make eye contact with the person who is most relevant to the particular point you're making at the time: go with this instinct.

Exercise 13 – Eye contact practise 2

You should also spread your eye contact around the whole of your audience: if you just focus on one side of the room, the other side will feel left out.

> • As an add-on to the above exercise, once you've finished your 5 seconds speaking to person A, rather than moving to person B next to them, look instead to person H, at the other side of the room.

> • Then look to person D, back at the centre of the room.

> • And so on, making sure you pay attention to all parts of the room.

> • This will feel uncomfortable and off-putting at first, but with practise you'll soon be able to do this naturally.

A mistake many people make is to work their way along the line, speaking at one person, then their neighbour, then their neighbour, and so on, like knocking down dominoes in a row. This looks unnatural, so you should avoid this at all costs. Sharing your eye contact around the room can feel forced or unnatural at first, but with a bit of practise you'll find yourself able to do it with little effort.

Aim to spend at least 80% of your time looking around the room, holding eye contact, etc., with less than 20% (ideally much less) glancing at your notes. This may sound daunting, but with plenty of practise it's definitely achievable.

Hands

One of the hardest parts of public speaking is knowing what to do with your hands. It's very common. Normally you wouldn't give them much thought, but as soon as you stand up in front of a group of people your hands feel like they've turned into two big slabs of meat, which you are far too aware of.

Some people say you should keep them rigid and still, others advise having something in your hand so you don't appear quite so uncomfortable. My advice is:

> • Relax: let your hands do whatever feels natural.

• Avoid holding anything. This can be extremely distracting, leaving your audience to wonder whether you are going to spill that glass of water, or making them feel like you're conducting them like an orchestra with your pen. If your hands shake when you're nervous then holding something can just draw attention to that.

• Keep your hands in plain view: if the audience can't see them, they'll wonder what you're doing with them. This particularly goes for putting your hands in pockets: sorry guys!

• Some people feel most comfortable holding on to the corner of a table, lectern or other piece of furniture. Try not to do this, as it can make you appear weak and uncertain, like a little schoolboy clinging onto the side of a desk for support. If you do find yourself holding on to something, keep it relaxed and light. A white knuckle grip not only tenses up your whole body but will also be very obvious to your audience.

Exercise 14 – Your hands

The following exercise will help you to relax your hands and free you to worry about other things:

> • Stand in a relaxed posture: whatever feels most comfortable to you. We'll be talking about how to plant your feet and legs in the next section, but don't worry about that for now: just focus on the top half of your body.

> • Don't forget to keep a straight back, chin up, and chest out as before.

> • Hold your arms out at 90 degrees from your body.

> • Shake your hands as violently as you can, as though you're trying to shake your fingers loose from the rest of your body.

> • (Note that this is just for the purposes of loosening up, finding what works for you and helping you practise. I wouldn't advise going through this routine in full view of the audience before you speak, as it might look a bit odd. If you find this exercise helpful and want to do it just before you speak, find somewhere private and out of the way to do so.)

> • Let your arms drop to your sides and let your hands fall so that they rest lightly on your thighs.

> • Keep them there to start with, but as you speak allow them to move should you feel the need: such as a gesture to accentuate a point. Keep it natural and in tune with what feels right to you.

> • If at any point you find yourself wondering what to do with them, return your hands to their original position, resting lightly on your thighs.

Include this in your practise routine. This way you should get a good feel for what works by the time you come round to standing up for real.

Feet

Usually at a wedding the speakers are behind the top table, so you don't need to worry about whether you should move or pace around or not: the layout decides this for you.

However, the way you stand can have a big impact on how you feel and come across. You don't want to be too rigid and come across as too tense; but you also don't want to be too relaxed and create a bad impression.

Exercise 15 – Standing

To give you an idea of how you should try to stand, have a go at the following exercise:

- Stand up with your feet a shoulder width apart

- Bend your knees a few times, bouncing on your heels and then the balls of your feet. Allow your legs to loosen up. Think about how golfers get ready to line up a shot.

- Settle to a standing position with your knees slightly bent (at least, not locked into place).

- In this resting position, you should be standing on the whole of your feet, distributing your weight evenly between your heels, balls of your feet and your toes.

- Practise this a few times so that the position you end up in comes to you naturally. You want to start off your speech in this position (probably without the loosening exercises, as that would again look a bit strange to your audience...).

12.4 Timing

A key part of delivering your speech is doing so in a measured, easy to follow way.

In the context of wedding speeches (or indeed any kind of public speaking), timing is about making sure you speak at the right pace, pausing in the right places, and keeping things flowing in a nice, interesting way.

Pace

In terms of pacing yourself, this is a bit of a balancing act:

> • Not too slowly that you end up sounding really boring or bored!

> • Not too fast that you tire people out, or they can't follow you.

When most people are nervous (i.e. speaking in front of a room of people) they have a tendency to speed up the pace of their words. Everything comes out in a mad jumble, as though they want to get done as quickly as possible. If you do this then you're guaranteed to be done quicker, but most people won't actually understand what you said.

There are a few things you can do to get the best pace:

> • Record yourself reading your speech aloud and listen back to it. You may be surprised at how fast you sound. If so, take a note and make a conscious effort to slow down.

> • Ask for feedback from others on how you sound.

> • Bear in mind your research on your audience (chapter 5). For example, if a proportion of your audience has English as their second language then you may need to speak slower and clearer than usual to ensure they can follow what you're saying.

> • On the day itself, you may find it helpful (especially if you have a habit of talking too quickly) to have someone in the audience with the task of signaling you if you're going too fast (or too slow) for comfort. Ideally they should stand at the back of the room so they're easy for you to spot; but also don't distract the rest of the audience if they do need to start waving at you!

Pauses

Using regular, well timed pauses can also be a good way of keeping your pace in check, especially if you have a tendency to speak too fast. They also give you an opportunity to take a breather, gather your thoughts and maybe have a quick drink of water.

Key things to bear in mind are:

• The pauses should be as natural as possible and not too frequent. Pausing after every sentence will slow you down too much and make the audience restless and impatient for you to get on with it.

• A pause can be seen as a cue for the audience to react (clap, laugh, etc.), so pick them carefully.

• Leave a gap which feels natural. This will depend on whether you're waiting for a reaction or not. As a general rule, no more than 5 seconds of complete silence at most (not counting if people are clapping, etc.).

• Don't be afraid to pause slightly longer than feels comfortable to you. Things usually feel more intense when you're standing up in front of others, and the chances are that what feels like an age to you won't feel half as long to those watching. If in doubt, practise and ask for feedback, making a mental note of what works and what doesn't.

Key places to pause are:

• After each joke.

• When you've said something requiring a reaction, such as when you want applause.

• If you've said something which you want the audience to think about.

• When you're changing subjects, or have come to the end of an anecdote. This gives the audience a chance to absorb what you've said and get ready for the change in subject.

• If you're using prompt cards (see chapter 11 for more on these), the end of each card is a handy place to pause. You can use this time to glance at the following card to remind you what you will be saying next; this will feel perfectly natural to you and your audience.

12.5 Using microphones

It may be that the wedding you're speaking at will have microphones to help you be heard loud and clear by the audience. If so, I still recommend that you learn and practise the above points on projection: if only as a back-up in case the microphones fail.

Even if you have a microphone you should make sure you speak clearly: a mumble through a microphone is just a mumble projected through a speaker.

Microphones can be deadly instruments in the hands of the inexperienced, with feedback being a particular risk. This is the horrible squealing sound you sometimes hear when someone picks up a microphone or stands too close to a speaker.

You should therefore make sure that you have the opportunity to practise with the actual microphone and set-up you'll be using, even if this is just a few minutes before everyone enters the room to sit down. Practise holding it in various ways to find out which is most comfortable for you while also picking up your voice in the best way. Make sure someone's on hand who knows how to operate the speaker system: it may be that you need to change the volume or other settings to find something which works for your voice.

A bit of time invested here really will pay dividends. And don't forget the projection techniques mentioned above: what would be more impressive than the microphone failing and you not being fazed, able to deliver a clear speech without it?

Delivery: Summary of main points

• Deep, regular breaths can help your projection as well as calm you down.

• Also keep a tall, straight posture.

• Keep eye contact with your audience as much as you can.

• Make your delivery nice and measured, with pauses at regular intervals.

***

Chapter 13 - Props

Many people will use props as a way of adding interest to their speech, making it different and memorable, and (for those less comfortable with public speaking) taking the focus away from them standing up there.

This could be something which illustrates the punchline of a joke, such as one of the groom's Hawaiian shirts maybe, or an inflatable sheep and a set of handcuffs to show people what happened on the stag do. On the other hand it could be a joke in itself: for example the old favourite where the best man talks about how, now he's settled down, the groom's days of sleeping around are over. Putting a hat on the table, he invites everyone who's been given a key to the groom's house to return it. Cue a stream of women and men (forewarned and provided with props in advance) coming forward to drop off keys into the hat.

Used properly, props can be great fun. However, there are a number of pitfalls and points to bear in mind if you are planning on using them in your speech.

Road test them

Just as you would with any other jokes, make sure you test your routine on as many people as possible. This is firstly to check that it is actually funny and appropriate, but also to ensure that it really does work. This is even more important given that anything involving props will stand out from the rest of your speech: a one-line joke which falls flat can be glossed over, but a routine with props that fails is very noticeable.

Practise, practise, practise

I've mentioned a few times the importance of practise. With props you should rehearse your routine over and over so that by the end you've ironed out every last kink and are 100% comfortable with it. This may be tedious, but it will pay dividends on the day. This applies no matter how short or simple the routine may be: it's amazing how sometimes the simplest things can be the ones which mess up the most.

Have a back-up plan

A real risk with using props is that they can fail (especially if technology is involved: see below). Make sure you have at least one back-up plan. Ideally you should have a replacement copy of whatever prop you're using, and also have some words prepared in case your props fail completely. You don't need to have a whole back-up speech prepared: as long as your speech hangs together without the props (that is, there aren't loads of references to them later in the speech) then you can just miss them out completely. Remember, you're the only one who has your speech in front of you: no-one else will notice if what you say isn't exactly how you planned.

Don't overcomplicate things

Given that using any sort of props increases the risk that something will go wrong, keep them as simple as possible. The more complicated your props are (whether that's to use or describe them), the more likely it is that things will go wrong. Or, just as bad, you'll spend so much time focusing on your props in your preparation that you neglect the rest of your speech. That brings us to...

Don't forget about the spoken bit!

Remember that a speech is mainly about you talking and telling them a story. Jokes or stories which use props to help illustrate them are a useful way to add a bit of interest, but they shouldn't take over the whole thing. This applies to the speech itself (you're doing a speech, not a magic show) and also – especially – your preparation and practise time.

Does it flow?

Don't get carried away with how hilarious your props-based gag is. Think about it in the context of your overall speech. Ask yourself if it adds something, or emphasises a point you're making. If the answer's "no" to either of these questions, then take it out. Be ruthless: a pointless gag can undermine the rest of your speech.

Get help

Don't be afraid to ask for help in actually doing your props routine: in fact I'd actively encourage you to do so. Getting someone to help can not only reduce the risk of something going wrong, but also gives you one less thing to worry about: give them the responsibility of making sure the props work, while you focus on your speech.

Room layout

Make sure you check that the room is suitable for the props you're planning. For instance, if you want to do a slide show, check that there's somewhere for the projector, a nearby power supply, and that everyone will be able to see clearly. Don't just assume all will be OK; make sure you check and double-check. If you can, go and check out the room in advance to make sure that what you're planning will definitely work.

Beware of the machines

There's an old saying from the movies that you should avoid working with children and animals. To this I would also add technology. Call me a fuddy-duddy technophobe if you want, but my experience is that as soon as you throw technology onto the mix you massively increase the chances of something going wrong.

To give you an example, I was once at a wedding where the best man's speech was centred around a collection of PowerPoint slides he was to project onto a screen and then talk to. He thought he'd covered all the bases, had brought his laptop with the slides pre-loaded, checked that the hotel had a screen and projector set up and waiting. However, he didn't bother to try connecting his laptop to the projector until just before it was his turn to speak.

You guessed it: they weren't compatible and he ended up spending 10 minutes sweating over the equipment in front of all the guests. There was amusement at first, followed by boredom, irritation and then everyone just started talking amongst themselves. When he finally gave up, he had not only lost the audience's focus but, because his speech had been based around the slides, he had nothing to say.

If you do decide to use something like this, learn from the above lesson and think very carefully about whether you really need to use technology or whether something else would work just as well. Never underestimate the power of the spoken word. If your answer is still "yes", then check that everything works and have a back-up plan ready, and also have something to say which doesn't rely on your props. Also have someone with you who is responsible for making sure it's all set up and working before you start speaking.

Props: Summary of main points

- Always have a back-up plan.

- Practise, practise and practise again to ensure that you're fully familiar with your props and how they work.

- Keep them as simple as possible.

- Get others to help you out.

- Don't let the props take over the whole thing – they should supplement your speech, not replace it.

***

Chapter 14 - Now That You've Finished...

You're now all set and ready to make your speech.

To recap what we've gone through:

In chapter 2 we thought about each of the speeches: what they should include, when they should be and how long. The main message here being that short is best.

In chapter 3 we considered the dreaded nerves, and looked at ways to make sure they don't ruin your day, including breathing and visualisation techniques.

In chapter 4 we covered the main things to think about before you start planning your speech, and in chapter 5 we widened this to include identifying your audience, so you could ensure your speech was suitable and more likely to be successful.

In chapter 6 we looked into the various ways you could get material for your speech, and in chapter 7 we pulled these together into a first draft speech.

Chapter 8 talked you through editing that first draft, which is supplemented by keeping on practising: chapter 9.

In chapter 10 we covered the key things you'll be expected to do on the day, as well as the speech.

In chapter 11 we looked at the two key ways you could have and use your notes when you do your speech: prompt cards and written notes.

In chapter 12 we covered the key ways to deliver your speech effectively, projecting your voice in a clear and understandable way.

Finally, in chapter 13 we looked at the things to bear in mind if you do use props in your speech.

Peter Oxley

Remember to also look through the Troubleshooting section at the end of this book if you have any specific questions or there are any areas you're still not comfortable with. If you're still stuck after reading this, then feel free to leave a message on my website www.perfectweddingspeech.com - I'll aim to get back to you as soon as I can.

Once you've done your speech and are settling back to reality, basking in the glow of a job well done, please do leave me a message on my website (www.perfectweddingspeech.com) to let me know how it went. In particular I'd welcome any feedback - good or bad - on how helpful or otherwise you found this guide. I'm always looking for ways to improve and your comments really are valued.

Good luck!

***

Chapter 15 - Troubleshooting

Contents:

A) What if I can't think of anything to say?

Chapters 6 and 7 should give you plenty of possibilities to ensure that you don't come up against a complete brick wall. I truly believe that, given a reasonable amount of time, anyone can pull together enough material to produce a good speech.

To recap, try the following:

• Keep a notebook with you to record any ideas as and when they come to you.

• Ask friends and family for ideas. Don't be afraid to bribe them with food or alcohol to help jog their memories.

• Brainstorm, asking yourself questions about your subject and jot down whatever comes to mind.

• You may also find mind maps a useful way of generating lots of ideas quickly.

• Hit the Internet, taking some key themes for inspiration (such as their hobbies, birth date, name, etc.).

• Don't forget other research sources, such as libraries, trade magazines and newspapers.

***

B) What if I can't start writing?

This is often because there's something more interesting or worthwhile to do: like going out, watching TV or doing the washing up. If that's the case, I'm afraid you're just going to have to force yourself to sit down somewhere quiet, with no distractions, and get on with it.

If it's the beginning of the speech that's causing you problems, try starting at the middle or even the end. You can then go back to write your opening lines when you've got into the flow of writing and maybe have a better idea of what to write.

You may also find it helps to use someone else to motivate you here: get them to keep checking on how you're doing, maybe even not allowing you to leave your desk until you're finished!

Chapter 7.7 also gives some tips on how to beat the dreaded Writers' Block, and the sample speech outlines at chapter 7.4 may also be helpful in giving you a framework to start you off.

***

C) What if my speech is too long?

When making a wedding speech you need to ensure that you don't overstay your welcome. Although they'll want to hear what you have to say and be entertained, the audience will get restless and bored if you go on for too long.

You should ask other people, particularly the organisers and the other speechmakers, what length of speech you should go for. If in doubt, err on the side of making it shorter rather than longer.

If you think that your speech is too long, try the following:

• Have another look at the tips on editing in chapter 8 and apply these again to your speech.

• You may need to think about the "big picture". If your speech is a lot longer than you'd like, then it's not enough to just cut out the odd word here or there: you need to lose whole sections to really have an impact on the length of your spoken speech.
• Are there any weak points in your speech you could cut out and not miss? If so, remove them.

• Strip it down to the bare essentials. What are the key points that you're trying to make? There shouldn't be too many of these: between three to five as a rough guide. Look through your speech and ask yourself which parts don't relate to these key points: and delete them. If this doesn't give you enough to delete, think about your key points: could you remove one or two of them?

• Ask for help: read out your speech to other people and ask them to point out sections that they don't think work.

• Be ruthless: your speech should be direct and to the point, and it may be that a certain story you absolutely love is the one to be removed. Novelists and other writers have a rule when editing their books: if there's a part of their draft work they are so in love with that it has to stay in, then that's the first thing to be deleted (they call it "killing the darlings"). Sometimes you can be so attached to an idea that you lose sight of whether it's actually any good or not.

***

D) What if my speech is too short?

The first question to consider is whether it really is too short. I personally would rather have (and listen to) a short, direct and to the point speech than one which rambles on for hours.

However, if you really do think that your speech is far too short, consider the following:

> • Look back over the things you should include in your speech (chapters 2 and 7). Is there anything here that you've missed?

> • Go back over your research notes and consider if there are any points or stories that you could include. Don't just add something for the sake of adding it. Whatever you add should be relevant and add something to the overall speech: whether it be humour, or an interesting insight into the person you're talking about.

> • Also look at A) What if I can't think of anything to say?

***

E) What if I decide my speech is rubbish?

You can protect against this by starting to write your speech as far in advance as possible and doing plenty of practise to iron out any kinks.

It's only natural to have these thoughts as you go through the process of writing and editing your speech: it's just the nerves kicking in. So the first thing to do is not to panic. If you've still got plenty of time before the day itself:

> • Take some time out. After a break of a few days, chances are it won't seem as bad as you thought.

> • Ask for help: someone else with fresh eyes may be able to spot issues and suggest improvements.

> • Ask yourself: Why are you worried? Is it just one bit (in which case, just strip out that bit and either remove it or rework it), or is it the speech as a whole? Either way, following the above two tips will help here.

If you're having these thoughts at the last minute, chances are it's just nerves kicking in, and it's actually not as bad as you thought. I'd definitely recommend against trying to do a complete rewrite of your speech just before you're due to deliver it. Nor should you let it ruin your night before the wedding: not being rested enough is almost as bad as not being prepared. In any event, remember to keep this in perspective: see chapters 2, 3 and 10 for some thoughts on this.

***

F) What if my speech is boring?

First of all, consider why you think it's boring. Take a break from it for a few days so you can come back to it with fresh eyes, and ask other people for their opinion.

If it's a question of just being too long, then see "C) What if my speech is too long?"

If it's the right length but you still think it's boring:

> • Consider injecting more personal content.

> • Consider adding more humour.

> • If the problem is a specific section, can you delete it? Or is there another way to present it so that it's more interesting: for instance, getting some audience involvement, shortening it or using some sort of props?

***

G) What if my speech doesn't flow or make sense?

See chapter 7 for guidance on how to make your speech flow.

If you find yourself struggling with an unstructured speech:

> • Take some time out to refresh your mind and so that you can come back to your speech with fresh eyes.

> • Break the speech down into its key sections and write these down as headings on a piece of paper. Looking at it fresh in this way, without the distraction of the content itself, consider whether there are any obvious links which you are missing.

> • Is it the whole speech or just some specific section which is unstructured? There's no point doing a wholesale rewrite if you don't need to.

> • Ask for another person's opinion. Often you'll find that someone else can quickly spot something you may miss as you're too close to what you've written.

> • Don't be afraid to be ruthless and tear your speech apart and then rebuild it. This can be a drastic step (and only to be done if you have plenty of time), but it can lead to huge improvements.

***

H) What if the speech before mine is really successful? How do I follow that?

First of all you should remember that this isn't a competition. You all have your own role to play and each speech is just as important as all the others.

Bear in mind as well that every speech is expected to do something different. See chapters 2 and 11 for a reminder of the roles of each speech and speechmaker.

One way to avoid any direct comparisons is to space the speeches out, rather than having one immediately after the other. For instance, at my wedding we had a speech after each course of the meal. This meant that enough time had passed between my father-in-law's frankly excellent speech and my own effort for me to not feel under pressure to be even funnier than him. It also reduced the risk of people getting "wedding speech fatigue": boredom from being bombarded with speech after speech without a break.

If you do find yourself following an amazing speech, start by acknowledging how good the previous speech was: this will strike a chord with the audience and show them that you're entering in the right spirit. You could also turn it into a joke: pretending that, because the previous one was so good, you're just going to give up on even trying to make a speech (e.g. stand up, look to the previous guy, shake your head, shrug to the audience then sit down, pretending to throw your notes away).

***

I) What if one of the earlier speeches uses some of my material?

Before you start to write you should speak to all the other speechmakers, to make sure that you don't end up making the same speech, or use the same stories. Remember, you're all in this together and a bit of forward planning can avoid a lot of last minute issues.

A lot of the points under "H) What if the speech before mine is successful?" also apply here, so it's worth having a look at that.

If you do find yourself sitting through someone else saying what you were going to say, then the first thing to consider is whether it really is the same. Remember that every speech plays a different role and every person has a different perspective on things: your version of a story may bring out a totally different point to someone else's telling of it.

If the story in question is a key part of your speech then you have no choice but to press on as planned, perhaps with a joke about how they're hearing it again. Try not to repeat any details that they've already heard: just provide a short summary instead.

If it's not essential to your speech, consider deleting it completely. Don't worry about finding something else to replace it: no-one else will know that your speech isn't quite as long as you'd planned. And after all, remember that shorter is definitely better when it comes to wedding speeches.

***

J) What if I lose my notes?

On the day itself you should be ultra-paranoid when it comes to your notes. Don't let them out of your possession, even for one minute.

Make multiple copies of the speech and keep them in separate places: maybe one in your pocket, one in your suitcase and another with a friend.

The biggest prevention and cure is practise though. If you've put in the hours before the day, then you'll probably find that you don't really need your notes anyway!

If you do lose your notes, and with no back-ups to hand, the first thing to do is not to panic. Keep it all in perspective: it won't ruin the whole day. There are worse things that could happen (see chapters 2, 3 and 10).

When you're feeling sufficiently calm, take yourself somewhere quiet and ask yourself whether you can replicate some or all of your speech from memory. If you've been practising then this should be fairly easy: don't try to reproduce the whole thing word-for-word; as long as you have the main themes then you have something to work with.

Also, speak to the other speechmakers and/or other guests and enlist their help. These situations always bring out the best in people and you'll probably be pleasantly surprised by what you can achieve with a little help.

Make sure you stick with something which is familiar to you. Trying to talk to unfamiliar material off-the-cuff is just a recipe for panic and, ultimately, disaster.

If all else fails, just cover the basics: introduce yourself, thank a few people, complement the bride on how she looks, raise a toast, and then sit down.

Don't give up. I really recommend going for it and trying to either do the speech from memory or ad libbing it. You'll get a lot more credit (and a sense of achievement) from doing this, rather than just throwing in the towel. What's the worst that can happen? You run out of things to say, toast the happy couple and sit down. I guarantee people will appreciate you at least making the effort and doing something they would be scared of doing.

***

K) What if I forget my props, or they don't work?

As mentioned in chapter 13, make sure you put in plenty of practise to iron out any kinks in your routine.

Have a back-up set of props ready just in case anything happens to your original one. Ideally keep them in a different place to the originals (or have someone else look after them) to reduce the risk of you forgetting both.

Task a friend with getting the props set up and ready to go: ideally long before the speeches are due to start.

Assume that the worst will happen and have a back-up plan ready, even if it's just skipping to the next section of your speech.

If the worst does happen, make a joke of it. Whatever you do, don't allow yourself to get flustered or angry. Sometimes a prop or trick going wrong can actually be funnier than one going right, as fans of the late, great, British comedian Tommy Cooper will confirm.

If your props are taking more than a minute or so to set up in front of the audience, then give up and move on: you'll quickly lose the audience's attention otherwise.

***

L) What if people interrupt or heckle me?

It's all too easy to assume the worst of your audience, but bear in mind that this is very unlikely to actually happen. Where people do shout something out, it is much more likely to be good-natured banter than a personal attack. Remember, you're talking at a family celebration, not a grimy comedy club.

In any case, even if they do heckle you, the audience is guaranteed to be more on your side than the heckler's. Therefore, as long as you deal with it in the right manner, you'll be fine.

If you have genuine cause to believe that someone is likely to cause trouble (probably because of who they are: an attention seeker or a noisy drunk, for example), then once you've identified them you have a few options to ensure they behave themselves:

> • Have a quiet word with them (or get a mutual friend to do this, depending on who they're most likely to listen to). Explain to them that this is a special day, the bride's happiness is of paramount importance, and it would be much appreciated if they'd save any banter for the bar, after the speeches are over.

> • Depending on how they'd react, it may also help to play on their conscience: tell them how nervous you are and how much you're dreading anyone putting you off your stride by heckling. I'd recommend you do this in private: a plea in front of their mates may just act as a red rag to a bull.

> • If you can, arrange to have them placed as far away from you as possible, so you're less likely to be distracted by them.

> • It may also be worth getting other people to help by keeping an eye on the potential offender: either to stop them drinking heavily, to shush them if they start to make comments, or to whisk them out of the room if they really do get out of hand.

• You can also structure your speech to reduce the risk of heckles: avoiding any subjects which may encourage comments, keeping a steady flow in your speech (although don't be afraid to use effective pauses in the right place), or using the audience's applause to drown out any potential heckles.

• The beginning of your speech (before you've got into your flow, and the audience is still sizing you up) is where you're most at risk of being heckled. Remember the tricks for generating applause and goodwill: complement the bride, say lots of "thank you"s and have a killer opening joke.

But what if you find yourself standing there and someone starts to heckle you? Here are some tips:

• Have a ready-made list of responses as a back-up.

• Make sure you don't personally attack the heckler: this will just lose you the audience's goodwill.

• It helps to not be too over-reliant on a script: give yourself the freedom to pause or improvise. This is where prompt cards really come into their own (see chapter 11).

• Ignore them and keep on going, remembering that you're the one in charge: not them. This approach should be used with care. You should acknowledge that you've heard their comment but have decided to ignore it, otherwise you risk them assuming you didn't hear and repeating themselves. A little smile or nod in their direction should be enough.

• Try playing on the audience's sympathy. Remember, they'll be on your side anyway, so even a nervous laugh and a plea for no more heckles may get just the response you want.

***

M) What if no-one laughs?

It's a recurring nightmare for people who stand up and try to make audiences laugh: what comedians call "dieing the death".

But is it really likely to happen, or is this just your paranoia kicking in? Few jokes are so bad that no-one will laugh at them. In fact, some jokes are so bad they're actually funny. Remember, the audience will be on your side, so they will laugh if you give them the chance, even if your jokes aren't the best ever told. They will be willing you to succeed.

They'll also be mindful of the fact that this is a wedding, not a comedy club. They're much more likely to support you than they would a professional comedian, for example.

Having plenty of personal content is the key here, something which is too often overlooked. If your speech is over-reliant on jokes and one-liners then there's an increased risk of some of them falling flat, mainly due to your audience having joke fatigue. So keep the jokes few and far between, and outnumber them with funny stories that actually happened, and are therefore directly relevant. At the very least, these will prompt laughs of recognition from those who were there at the time.

Make sure you road test all your jokes beforehand, firstly to check that they are actually funny and appropriate, but also to check that the way you tell them is funny.

Remember to avoid anything offensive or insulting: see chapter 5 on The Audience.

If you do find yourself in the horrible situation of having told a joke and been greeted by a wall of silence, here are some tips on how to deal with it:

> • Keep on going. Don't make the silence stretch out for longer than it needs to. This will just draw attention to the failed joke and make you feel that much worse.

• Don't take it personally. These things happen, and their response isn't a reflection on you. Like a prize fighter, pick yourself up, dust yourself down and chalk it down to experience.

• Make a joke of it. Have some lines ready as a back-up just in case. The comedian Eddie Izzard has a great way of dealing with lines that don't quite work: he pulls out an imaginary notebook and mimes writing something along the lines of "next time remember that joke's not funny..."

***

N) What if I offend people?

Do your homework on the audience (see chapter 5). Review your speech carefully and remove anything which could cause offence.

Enlist the help of others: ask for their opinions as to whether something is funny or just offensive.

If in any doubt about a particular piece, err on the side of caution and don't use it.

If you find yourself mid-way through your speech and having offended someone, you need to get the audience back onside as quickly as possible. The safest strategy is to apologise and then move on. Don't dwell on it or draw even more attention to it.

***

O) What if people can't hear or understand me?

Chapter 12 provides some tips on how to boost your projection and overall delivery.

Make sure you practise plenty, using someone else to provide a sounding board for your delivery.

Also try recording yourself doing your speech, with the microphone far enough away to simulate how you could sound to others. Force yourself to listen to / watch this recording, and learn from what goes well or not so well. Bear in mind that no-one enjoys seeing or hearing themselves talk, and we're all our own worst critic, so don't let this destroy your confidence.

As mentioned above, chapter 12 has plenty of tips on how to enhance your projection, but a key one to remember is breathing. It's a simple thing, but a few deep breaths at an opportune moment can really work wonders for your delivery.

Get a friend to stand at the back of the room, ready with a pre-arranged signal (or signals) to prompt you to raise your voice or slow down if at any point you happen to slip into bad habits.

***

P) What if I get nervous?

See chapter 3 on dealing with nerves for more detailed tips here. Below are a few key things to think about.

Keep it in perspective. Remember that the speeches are only one (small) part of the day.

Talk to people about how you feel. This will have two advantages: they may be able to help you get over a specific fear, and also the act of talking about our fears can often make them seem a little less overpowering.

Use the visualisation techniques outlined at chapter 3 to imagine a happy, stress-free outcome.

The best cure for nerves is to get up and start talking. This may sound harsh, but the approach of throwing yourself in at the deep end really does work. Force yourself to stand up, take a big, deep breath, and then throw yourself into your first lines. It'll be over before you know it: I promise.

***

Q) What if I lose my place when I'm talking?

I'm afraid it's my old favourite again: practise. The more you practise and the more comfortable you are with your material, the less likely you are to get lost.

You should also make sure your notes are clear and easy to follow: see chapter 11 for some tips in this regard.

If you find that you've lost your place when you're doing the speech:

> • First of all, don't panic. Forget about everything around you and just focus on remembering where you got to.

> • Don't be afraid to pause while you recover your flow. Any silence will seem longer to you than it does to the audience.

> • You could ask for help from your audience. Asking "Now, where was I?" will usually get good natured replies, and if you're smooth enough you can make it appear as though it were a part of your planned speech after all.

> • Try turning it into a joke, and have some back-up lines ready, just in case. A favourite of mine is: "Now we all have something in common: none of us knows what I'm going to say next!" While they laugh at this, you can use the break in pressure to find your place and then carry on.

***

R) What if people won't stop talking?

The traditional approach is to use a loud noise to announce that someone is about to speak, and this can be effective: whether it's a gavel on a table or even tapping your glass with a spoon. I'd recommend against trying to get their attention by shouting: even if you don't get drowned out in the general sound of voices, you'll risk sounding (and feeling) like a schoolmaster trying to control an unruly class of pupils: not the best start to your speech.

Saying something which will get people clapping or cheering is a good way to bring chatterboxes into line. Thanking the organisers, bridal party, etc., is a good way to achieve this.

Don't wait for the whole room to be silent. Once there are enough pockets of people paying attention then the rest will usually follow. As soon as there's enough quiet for you to be heard by some of the audience, start speaking: the remainder will soon be shushed by those who already realise you're speaking.

It's also worth taking a look at the points under "L) What if people interrupt or heckle me?"

***

S) What if I struggle over a certain section of the speech?

If, in your practice sessions, you constantly find yourself struggling with a certain part – maybe the words just won't come out right or you keep forgetting something – then this may be a very good sign that something's wrong with that section of your speech. Take another look at it and consider either rewording it or taking it out altogether. See chapter 8 on editing for more information on this.

If you stumble during the speech itself, then don't panic. Just plough on with your speech, maybe making a joke of it: e.g. "I'll put my teeth back in now…", or "I know what you're thinking – that's easy for me to say!"

***

T) What if the audience are all too conservative for the jokes I wanted to do?

Hopefully you'll realize this when you're doing your research and pulling together your speech, giving you enough time to amend it so it's suitable for your audience. See chapter 5 for what to consider in relation to your audience and making your speech suitable for them.

Ask for the opinions of other people on the suitability of your material. If you're in any doubt then you should err on the side of caution and not use it.

If you only realize this at the last minute, then give serious consideration to the relevant section of your speech. Could you remove it without harming your speech too much? Could you reword the offending section so that it doesn't cause offence, maybe changing the context or certain key parts? See chapter 8 on editing for more information on this.

If you've come to the realisation when it's far too late, then you're in damage limitation territory. See "N) What if I offend people?"

***

About the author

Peter Oxley is a business manager and freelance writer based in the English Home Counties.

As well as weddings and other social occasions, Peter has extensive experience of speaking in front of a wide range of audiences, including colleagues, boards of directors and militant workers, to name a few. He lives with his wife, two young sons and a slowly growing guitar collection. Probably a masochist: aside from writing and willingly speaking in front of large crowds of strangers, Peter spends his spare time playing music badly and supporting football teams that play badly.

This is his first published book.

Connect with me online

Twitter: www.twitter.com/peterdoxley

My blog: http//www.perfectweddingspeech.com

My author website: http//www.peterdoxley.co.uk

6359149R00082

Printed in Great Britain
by Amazon.co.uk, Ltd.,
Marston Gate.